THE MANKIND SERIES OF GREAT ADVENTURES OF HISTORY

The Birth of America

Compiled, edited and with an Introduction
by Raymond Friday Locke

A Mankind Book

MANKIND PUBLISHING COMPANY
LOS ANGELES

THE MANKIND SERIES OF GREAT ADVENTURES OF HISTORY

The Birth of America

"The Dutch Colonial Failure in New York," by Cecil B. Currey, © 1970 by Mankind Publishing Company.

"Meet Wiley and Micajah Harpe: Unkind Men," by G. G. Hatheway, © 1968 by Mankind Publishing Company.

"Benjamin West: The Quaker Rembrandt," by Robert Hardy Andrews, © 1968 by Mankind Publishing Company.

"The Aaron Burr Affair," by Robert Hardy Andrews, © 1967 by Mankind Publishing Company.

"William Duer and the Origins of the New York Stock Exchange," by Robert Sobel, © 1970 by Mankind Publishing Company.

"John Adams: The First Angry Man in the White House," by Robert Hardy Andrews, © 1969 by Mankind Publishing Company.

"The Ride A Nation Forgot," by Howald Baily, © 1969 by Mankind Publishing Company.

"The Sale of Alaska," by M. Belov, © 1967 by Mankind Publishing Company.

"Alaska: From Russia With Love," by David Lindsey, © 1967 by Mankind Publishing Company.

"The Secret History of Benedict Arnold," by Robert Hardy Andrews, © 1971 by Mankind Publishing Company.

© 1971 by Mankind Publishing Company, 8060 Melrose Avenue, Los Angeles, California. All rights reserved.

Library of Congress Catalog Card Number: 78-135911
SBN: 87687-007-8

Book design by Andrew Furr

CONTENTS

The Dutch Colonial Failure in New York by Cecil B. Currey	9
Meet Wiley and Micajah Harpe: Unkind Men by G. G. Hatheway	53
Benjamin West: The Quaker Rembrandt by Robert Hardy Andrews	85
The Aaron Burr Affair by Robert Hardy Andrews	101
William Duer and the Origins of the New York Stock Exchange by Robert Sobel	133
John Adams: The First Angry Man in the White House by Robert Hardy Andrews	149
The Ride a Nation Forgot by Howald Baily	179
The Sale of Alaska by Mikhail Belov	187
Alaska: From Russia With Love by David Lindsey	201
The Secret History of Benedict Arnold by Robert Hardy Andrews	217
Contributors	253

INTRODUCTION

One would probably expect a book carrying the title *The Birth of America* to be about the American Revolution but there was much more to the formation of the United States than that heroic effort on the part of the Colonists. The deeds of men—famous, infamous and some that have been forgotten—were also involved in the struggle for American freedom. The nine articles in this book were selected to throw a bit of light into a few dark corners of early American history. Cecil B. Currey tells us how the Dutch failed to hold New York and lost it to the English. Dr. G. G. Hatheway, in telling the story of Wiley and Micajah Harpe, who were two of the most evil murderers the frontier knew, has recreated the atmosphere of the America of the late eighteenth century. The profile of Benjamin West gives us some idea of the artistic world of the young republic and we learn from Robert Hardy Andrews' treatment of John Adams that violent dissent in Washington has been with us from the beginning. There are also two views of the American purchase of Alaska from Russian in this volume. M. Belov, an eminent Soviet historian, tells the story from the Russian viewpoint while a notable American scholar, David Lindsey, gives us the American side of the story. Also included in this volume is the story of the founding of the New York Stock Exchange, the strange tale of Benedict Arnold and the tale of one of the unsung heroes of American history, a young man named Jack Jouett.

RAYMOND FRIDAY LOCKE
Editor, Mankind Magazine

Along the canal in Dutch Manhattan. (Culver)

THE DUTCH COLONIAL FAILURE IN NEW YORK

by Cecil B. Currey

*W*rote Henry Hudson, a ship captain employed by the Dutch, early in the 17th century: "It is as beautiful a land as one can tread upon." He recalled the forests, meadows and waterways of the New World he had explored, one day to be known as New York. The words of Hudson were prologue. From the recently independent Netherlands ("low lands") came a burst of imperial energy that startled older nations. At their peak, the Dutch controlled great stretches of ocean. Atlantic passages became hazardous for ships of nations opposed by the Dutch. They wrested African slaving stations and much of Brazil from the Portuguese. Great plunders from the Spanish Main fell to the Dutch. The Netherlands hoisted its emblem above Caribbee isles and, in North America, a Dutch colony formed a wedge between the English colonies of New England and those of the Chesapeake area, as well as blocking French advance into that strategic location.

All this was squandered in fifty years. By 1664 the Dutch retained no holdings in continental America. In the Caribbean, save for a few dots of land, only Curacao remained. Spain retained her American possessions for over 300 years, England for nearly 170, France for over 150. But the Dutch effort was a failure. No solid base was constructed for a healthy growth of American colonies. Real advantages were wasted. Fortuitous circumstances were ignored which might have promoted development. And overshadowing all else was the unsuitable government controlling Dutch enterprises in America.

The rumblings of empire began with Hudson's voyage. An English seafarer and friend of Captain John Smith, Hudson sailed westward in 1609 in search of the water route to the Orient. If found, the Dutch could compete commercially with the Portuguese without entering the coastal waters of West Africa which their Iberian enemies still made dangerous for interlopers. The *Half-Moon* made landfall off the coast of America and Hudson soon located the river which now bears his name—over one hundred and fifty miles of navigable water leading to the Mohawk Valley, pathway to the West, and the wilderness fastness of the Iroquois confederacy. He called it the Mauritius after Prince Maurice. Others would long call it the North in contrast to the South (Delaware) River.

Hudson hoped this river might be the elusive water passage to India. By September, having sailed upriver to approximately the site of present day Albany, he realized this was not the "northwest passage." Hudson sailed back downriver and out into the bay—present day New York harbor—and past a sandbar now known as Sandy Hook into the open sea. He and his crew soon told of the riches available in the New World through the Indian fur trade.

Dutch contact continued; traders visited the area in 1610 and 1611. In 1612 merchants sent Adriaen Block on a voyage to the New World and he returned two years later. He named the strait of "Hellegat," or Hell Gate, the Connecticut River, Rhode Island, and Block Island. He was the first to realize that Manhattan and Long Island were not connected.

Dutch expansion continued in 1614 when burghers organized the New or United Netherland Company, chartered by the States-General. The Company's patent gave it a three year trading monopoly between Virginia and New France (the fortieth to fiftieth parallels). The Company had no power to establish settlements or to govern. Its activities still aroused the jealousy of other nations for its grant cut across lands claimed by France and England.

The Company sponsored a great deal of exploration but, despite this activity, failed to receive an extension of its monopoly. A successor to it was not found until June 3, 1621, when the States-General issued a patent incorporating the Dutch West India Company. This Company had vast powers. It received a twenty-four year monopoly on Dutch enterprise in America, and was to pit itself against Portuguese and Spanish domination of West Africa, Central and South America. The Company had power to conduct war, make peace, issue laws, administer justice, negotiate treaties with tribal chieftains—African and American—and appoint and remove officials. It was governed by a board of directors—the College of Nineteen. The Company's legal powers made it almost a state within a state.

The Company sent five families to the New World in 1621. The English government bitterly complained, calling them trespassers. The Company avoided the issue, claiming that trading was its only aim and it had no authority to plant a colony. This resentment, however, may have been the reason the Company delayed until 1624 before issuing its Provisional Order, or first plan of government for settlers in America.

Under this system, Company authority was exercised by the College of Nineteen through a resident Director-General, or governor, appointed subject to States-General approval. The Director-General was assigned almost despotic power. He could do nearly anything he wished short of inflicting capital punishment. In his own person, the governor possessed executive, legislative, and judicial powers. Directors-General thus had more authority than their English counterparts who were restricted by charters and representative assemblies. This made it necessary that governors be men of ability, tact, and force of character. Unfortunately, the Dutch West India Company often appointed men distinguished primarily by incompetence.

The governor was assisted by a five-man advisory council. Other officials were a *koopman* (bookkeeper of wages), a *schout fiscal* (attorney and sheriff), a *commis* or supercargo (assistant governor and superintendent of the fur trade). Colonists had no voice in their own governance. The Company believed absolute centralized control best for furthering its commercial purposes.

Spain also restricted her colonists, but in a more ordered fashion. Official arbitrariness was limited because the whole overseas effort was conducted as a government enterprise. The Spanish empire in America was an organic part of the government under the monarch. From the local *fray* and *conquistador* to the provincial *audiencia* and captain-general, from the viceroys of New Spain and Peru to the *casa de contratacion* and Council of the Indies, Spanish law, responsibility, and review prevailed.

England's colonies were at the opposite pole. Here general charters allowed for local initiative, representative assemblies, checks and balances. In these provinces, differing conditions brought forth divergent responses. English colonists at least could console themselves with the thought that they were—if not the masters—at least the shapers of their own fates. Importantly also, the profit seeking joint stock companies which founded certain English colonies gradually disappeared as their creations grew and matured.

The Dutch enterprise captured the worst of both Spanish and English worlds. From first to last their American colony was ruled by a private company, interested more in dividends than in provisioning settlers. The colony's settlers were ruled with a rigidity reminiscent of the Spanish empire but lacking that power's safeguards from caprice, pettiness, and tyranny. Spanish settlers were usually willing to put up with demands made upon them for they were ruled directly by the mother country.

The people of the Dutch colony were confined just as rigidly so that someone else could become rich. This they did not appreciate. Their joint stock company did not allow them the freedom English companies allowed their peoples, and settlers of the Dutch colony were not homogenous as were the inhabitants of Spanish provinces. All in all, the Dutch chose the worst possible bastardization of methods available for the establishment of colonies. From the beginning, the Dutch enterprise was doomed. Yet those who began, not being prophets, were hopeful.

The real beginning of New Netherland was in 1625 when Willem Verhulst came to the colony and platted several farms on Manhattan Island and began construction of Fort Amsterdam, located on the site known today as The Battery. This fort, when completed, was five-sided, guarded by a wide moat. A street divided the grounds, each end of which connected with a gate

The landing of Henry Hudson in 1609. (Culver)

Henry Hudson's interview with the Indians. (Culver)

in the palisade wall. Situated along the avenue were a marketplace, houses and offices of colonial leaders, school, church, warehouse, powder magazine, hospital and barracks for Company employees.

The population of the tiny colony soon increased slightly. On December 19, 1625, Pieter Minuit (sometimes spelled and hence probably pronounced as "Minnewit") and several others embarked for the New World aboard the *Sea-Mew*. Four and one-half months passed before the ship docked at Manhattan Island on May 4, 1626. The Company believed Verhulst to be incompetent, so in September he was replaced by Minuit. For several months after taking office, quarters within the fort remained incompleted, and so Minuit conducted his duties from a cabin on the *Sea-Mew*.

In 1625 or 1626 Negro slaves were first brought to New Netherland. Colonists learned that small grain farming was profitable. Crops of wheat and rye flourished. As early as 1626, exports brought in 45,000 guilders; by 1632 this total had risen to 125,000 guilders. The Company established farms, or *bouweries*. Five were laid out on the lower end of Manhattan for the Company and four others were carved out by its officials for themselves. Farm overseers, or *bouwmeisters*, guided the work of Company indentured servants, or *bouwlieden*. Further north, free settlers set up farms and sold or traded their surplus to other free colonists. The thrift, energy, and skill of those settlers soon made the lower end of the island bloom. The road north alongside these farms was soon known as the "farm road," or, as it is better known today, the *Bouwerie* ("Bowery"), on New York's lower East Side.

Minuit believed the colony's permanence depended on establishing friendly relations with nearby colonists from other nations and the Indians. He soon made close contact with the inhabitants of Plymouth colony. These Congregationalists appreciated their Dutch neighbors—remembering the kindness of Leyden townsfolk who had harbored them and who allowed them to worship in peace after they fled Scrooby Manor in England some years earlier under Stuart persecutions.

Nor were the Indians neglected. The explorer Champlain had long ago developed contacts with the Algonquins and had aided them against their enemies, the Iroquois. The French knew that if the Iroquois were conquered, it would open the shores of Lake Erie and Ontario, Champlain and George and the Mohawk Valley to French advance. But the Dutch sided with the Iroquois, provided them with guns, and around 1618 made a formal treaty with them, closing a large part of North America to the French. The Iroquois remained as a Dutch buffer against the French and later were used by the English during the Anglo-French conflict.

The Dutch West India Company, dependent upon the fur trade for its profits, wanted to cultivate the Indians. Minuit was told that "they must not be expelled with violence or threats, but be persuaded with kind words . . . , or otherwise should be given something for it (the land) to placate them." Thus one of Minuit's first acts was the purchase of Manhattan Island.

He gave, in exchange for the land, beads, ribbons, and other trinkets valued at sixty guilders ($24.00). Minuit estimated his purchase to be "eleven thousand margins in size and twenty-two thousand acres." The sum paid seems paltry today and undoubtedly Minuit congratulated himself on his bargain. It is also quite possible that the Indians laughed among themselves over the riches they had gained by giving strange men from across the sea rights to land they could have had for nothing. The interesting part of this transaction is not that Minuit paid so little, but that he paid at all. Most later settlers, as is well known, took Indian lands without any payment.

DUTCH COLONIAL FAILURE IN NEW YORK

By the close of 1626, New Amsterdam was a bustling, tiny village and the capital of New Netherland. No streets had been platted, however, and buildings sprang up helter-skelter while citizens strolled to their destinations by routes that pleased their fancy. Paths thus worn became permanent, the origin of the haphazard pattern of streets in lower New York City today.

The greatest act of Minuit's administration, perhaps the most significant of the Dutch period, was the establishment of religious liberty. Desperate for settlers, Minuit welcomed all who would come: Walloons (he was one himself), Huguenots, Lutherans, Baptists, Catholics, and others of still different religious persuasions. Persecution, so freely practiced elsewhere in both New and Old Worlds, was notably lacking.

Nationality also quickly became mixed. Besides the Dutch, there were Norwegians, Flemish, Swedes, Danes, Scots, Irish, English, Germans, Jews, and Negroes living in the colony. As early as 1643 when New Amsterdam was a bustling city of four hundred, eighteen languages were spoken there. The town was thus cosmopolitan from the first. The colony was, and the state of New York has ever since been, the "melting pot" of nations, religions, and political beliefs. Unfortunately, this same spirit of tolerance also contributed to a lack of group feeling and common loyalty which played havoc with the colony's integrity in the dark days of 1664 when the English challenge came. The colony was so constructed that even its victories and achievements seemed to hasten its decline.

Growth was tortuously slow. In 1627, appalled at the lack of population, the officers of the Dutch West India Company felt something new had to be tried to stimulate its settlement. Perhaps a baronial land system could provide a solid agricultural base in North America to supplement and complement Dutch efforts in the Caribbean, while costing the Company itself very little.

So it was that the board of directors issued, in 1629, the "Charter of Privileges and Exemptions."

This charter allowed any member of the Company certain privileges if he established a community of fifty persons over fifteen years of age in any part of New Netherland. Such a man was to adopt the title *patroon*, and to receive sixteen miles of land along one side of a navigable river or eight miles on both shores. Claims could extend inland as far as desired. Before a grant's confirmation, land must be purchased from the Indians. The island of Manhattan and the Indian fur trade were not to be infringed upon by patroons.

A patroon's settlers bound themselves (a) not to make woolen, linen, or cotton cloths, or to weave any other stuffs on threat of banishment, (b) to cultivate the patroon's land for ten years and not to leave it without permission, (c) to give the patroon first option to buy surplus produce, (d) to allow the patroon to settle small disputes in his court. Quarrels involving more than $20.00 value could be appealed to the Company (although patroons usually made settlers promise not to do so), (e) to have their grains ground by the patroon and to pay him for the costs involved, (f) not to fish or hunt on patroon property, and (g) if a settler died intestate, his property reverted to the patroon.

These rules doomed the patroon system. Unfortunately, the plan also prevented a free system of small farms which would have given strength and solidity to the colony. Tenants of patroons quickly became dissatisfied with their lot. The program itself was wrong. It was an effort to transplant to America a feudal land policy not even suited to existing Old World conditions. Men did not wish to bind their freedom so another might become a patroon, and life in Holland was such that few needed to emigrate.

The project also opened the door to corruption. While the patroon plan was being forged in the offices of the Company, several directors took advantage of their position. Through agents, they selected the choicest lands and their claims were ready the moment the plan was approved.

Such greediness disgusted many and the operation was shut down after but five patroonships had been granted. The van Cortlandts and Schuylers claimed large tracts. Michael Pauw got Staten Island and the present area of Jersey City. Samuel Godyn and Samuel Blommaert got an area approximately the size and location of the state of Delaware. Kiliaen van Rensselaer, a wealthy Amsterdam diamond and gold merchant, gained an estate of some seven hundred thousand acres near Albany. In blithe disregard of the rules, he claimed twenty-four miles on both sides of the Hudson River. Eventually these holdings grew until they were larger than present day Rhode Island and provided the basis for the large Hudson River estates which lasted well into the nineteenth century.

Godyn and Blommaert planted the community of Swannendael on the Delaware River in 1631, but it was destroyed by the Indians in the second year of its existence and abandoned. By 1635 they willingly sold their holdings to the Company. Pauw sold his claim to the Company in 1637. The only successful patroon was van Rensselaer. In 1640 the Company tried again, offering much reduced grants. The project was still unworkable. Further claims were prohibited in 1646 and an effort was made to repurchase all existing grants. By 1664, the Company regained all but two patroonships.

The first casualty of the patroon plan was Director-General Pieter Minuit. Believing he had helped those who "jumped the gun" in 1629, the Company recalled him. Minuit resigned and offered his services to Christiana, the Queen of Sweden. She sent him on an expedition to the Delaware where he started a settlement, New Sweden, and ruled it as governor for two years.

He whose responsibility New Netherland had been for seven years now established a competitor right next door. When even an ex-governor could find no lasting loyalty for the Dutch colony—how could *bouwlieden* be expected to do so?

Wouter van Twiller was Minuit's successor. His personal indecisiveness earned him the nickname "Wouter the Doubter," and as such he was immortalized in Washington Irving's *Knickerbocker History*. With van Twiller came a schoolmaster Adam Roelentsen. The Dutch were more concerned about the education of their children at this early date than many other people. By the end of the Dutch period, nine out of ten towns provided common schools for the young—the foundation of parochial schools upon which Roman Catholics built so solidly in later years.

The Dutch began extending the limits of their colony into the Delaware area and also the Connecticut Valley. They seemed well on their way to permanent settlement of the latter. However, both Puritan and Pilgrim felt that such penetration was a threat to them. Governor Winthrop of Massachusetts protested the moves of the "Hollanders." Complaints availed him exactly nothing. Whereupon a group from Plymouth colony migrated into the Connecticut. Good farming land there attracted other Bay area settlers. English numbers soon suppressed Dutch hopes and they finally withdrew. The basic weakness of the Dutch colony—lack of ability to maintain growth—had manifested itself.

Van Twiller may have been unable to expand the limits of New Netherland but he was quite successful in stretching his own holdings. He purchased Nut or Nutten Island and made his home there, so that it was shortly known as Governor's Island. His lands made him one of the larger real estate owners in the colony. Suspicious Company directors fired him in 1637 on charges of diverting their funds to his own use.

The Dutch West India Company came to feel that colonization of New Netherland was unprofitable compared with riches to be had elsewhere. Yet instead of revamping their approach to provide a sounder colonial structure, the Company continued the same heavy-handed policy, and—in a moment of absent-minded idiocy—chose the worst possible successor for van Twiller. When Willem Kiefft arrived in 1637, conditions in New Netherland were ruinous. Company employees were illegally trading in furs. Smuggling was common, gun sales to Indians had risen to dangerous proportions. The town was disorderly. Drunkenness, theft, fighting, mutiny, and homicide were everyday occurrences.

Kiefft issued proclamations almost without number: no furs were to be exported without his express permission; no one could sell powder to the Indians; all sailors must return to their ships by nightfall; fighting, rebellion, theft, perjury, and "all other immoralities" were forbidden. The governor decided when people should go to bed and get up, when they would go to work, and when they would quit. Because his edicts aroused so much antagonism, neither the habits nor morals of the colonists were appreciably changed.

Kiefft initially set an example of church-going. Soon the *domine*, or pastor, of the Dutch Reformed Church who had arrived in 1633 with Wouter van Twiller, Everardus Bogardus, found much to criticize. Bogardus bitterly assailed the governor's conduct of Indian affairs. He accused Kiefft of drunkenness and, from the pulpit, charged him with murder. Kiefft stopped attending services and induced others to do likewise. Denunciations thundered upon him from the pulpit. In retaliation, Kiefft ordered drums beaten and cannon fired during worship to distract those in attendance.

Kiefft may have been right in his belief that Bogardus was a wretch, but there is no room for doubt of Bogardus' assessment that Kiefft's Indian policy was a murderous one. New England often engaged in Indian wars but the Dutch made an active attempt to maintain peace with the natives. Kiefft's administration was an exception. From 1641 to 1645, the Indians killed between one and two thousand settlers and made life inhospitable for all who lived beyond the immediate vicinity of Fort Amsterdam.

Even there one's safety was often precarious. For better defense, the Director-General caused a wooden fence, or wall, to be erected on the northern edge of town. The path worn along its inner side was soon known as Wall Street, and has been so known ever since. People could go out through a gate to their *bouweries* toward the north when it was safe to do so. This path to the farms became the Broadway of modern New York City. The Dutch complained bitterly because often it was unsafe to venture beyond the wall.

In 1641, Kiefft called together leading settlers to consider the best course of action to take against the Indians. Out of this conference came a move for popular participation in government. The Council of "Twelve Men," chosen to advise the governor, urged popular representation and control of the official council. Infuriated, Kiefft immediately dismissed them, the first popular assembly called in New Netherland.

Escalation of the war in 1643, however, forced Kiefft to call another meeting from which emerged a second group of advisors known as the "Eight Men." The Eight, like the Twelve, soon found themselves at odds with the governor. Their leader was Adriaen van der Donck, owner of the patroonship Colen Donck (Yonkers). The Eight complained that Kiefft's handling of the Indians had caused their fields to "lie fallow and waste; our dwellings and other buildings . . . burned . . . we have no means to provide necessaries for wives or children; and we sit here amid thousands of barbarians, from whom we find neither peace nor mercy."

The war did not end until 1645. The loss in human life was staggering. In 1646, there were but fifteen hundred in the colony and as late as 1650 there were but two thousand inhabitants, half of whom were English immigrants. So desperate was the need for settlers that a call was put out for anyone whether he be "noble or ignoble, freeman or slave, debtor or creditor, yea, to the lowest prisoner included."

Willem Kiefft was recalled in 1647 and Pieter Stuyvesant came from Curacao to rule over a discouraged people. A clergyman's son, Stuyvesant was a tall, dark man of fifty-five. He carried himself like a prince and swore like a pirate. He had served the Company for years as a soldier, and had lost his right leg in a fight with the Portuguese at Curacao. His wooden peg, decorated with silver bands and nails gave him his nickname: Old Silver Nails. He stumped ashore determined to bring order. He greeted the five hundred people of the town: "I shall govern you as a father does his children." Accustomed to command and to unquestioning obedience, he saw no reason to delay in enforcing his rule.

Little New Amsterdam was as vicious and disordered a seaport as any along the Atlantic. Piracy and smuggling flourished as did illicit sales of guns and liquor to the Indians. Upcountry, Rensselaerswick and other manor estates in the Hudson and Connecticut valleys were operated in open defiance of Company rules. On Long Island, Dutch influence was disappearing as English settlers crowded in.

As Kiefft had done before him, Stuyvesant began a wholesale crusade against the disorder. Drunkenness and swearing were made illegal. Taverns were brought under supervision. Minor crimes were punished by public flogging. Felons were sent to the gallows with dispatch. Sales of liquor and weapons to Indians became punishable by death. Streets were straightened. To make the area more habitable, pigs and chickens were cooped up, rubbish thrown into the sea.

The solid Dutch burghers must have been gladdened by these efforts. New Netherland became more like their old home across the sea. The capital, which in 1643 had had but four hundred people, grew until in 1656 there were one hundred and twenty houses and one thousand persons. By 1660 there were three hundred and fifty houses and an additional five hundred persons. A chimney tax was levied in 1657 to pay for a fire patrol. The following year a police force was established. Some streets were paved.

Cleanliness became commonplace. As in the old country, shoes were left outside before one entered a home and, in the inns, owners shed their clogs before showing guests to their chambers. The town's houses became more attractive. Most were still constructed of wood although a few brick houses appeared, with gable ends facing the street, steep tiled roofs, large divided doors, little windows, and floors sanded and scrubbed.

Toward the north, along the dusty *Bouwerie*, small farmhouses and neat fields appeared with increasing frequency. Farmlands bloomed, little communities were garlanded with orchards. South of the wall, the Reformed Church and the fort were rebuilt. And the legends and myths ever since associated with Dutch New York began to take shape.

All up and down the Hudson from Tappan Zee to Fort Orange and up into the Catskills, every hollow and inlet had its special story. An early tale concerned a Negro pirate whom Stuyvesant had supposedly shot with a silver bullet at Hell Gate. On dark, misty nights, the "Pirate's Spook" could be seen, wearing his three-cornered hat, standing in the stern of his jollyboat. In the hill country there were those who saw a headless horseman riding through the night with his head under his arm. The trolls could be heard at their everlasting bowling, and perhaps Rip Van Winkle's grandfather was already looking lovingly at his wife and hoping for a son.

Stuyvesant's reign was not as idyllic as this might indicate. He provided needed stability but all his measures were carried out with so little tact that he aroused great antagonism. Additionally, chronic poverty plagued the province. Funds should have been provided by the Company, but that had never been its way. It had decided that warring and piracy against Spain and Portugal were more profitable. Even in 1627, when Admiral Piet Pieterszoon Heyn had captured the Spanish silver fleet of Matanzas in Cuba, the directors declared a dividend rather than investing this windfall in New Netherland. Small initial stock subscriptions and unwise business practices forced the Company into bankruptcy by 1645. Whereas earlier the Company had chosen to ignore its colony, now it was forced to do so. For New Netherland, it was "root hog, or die."

Stuyvesant knew that needed money would be raised locally or not at all. He felt colonists would be more tractable if they had a voice in raising and spending taxes. In the fall of 1647, Stuyvesant ordered eighteen men to be chosen from various communities from which he picked "Nine Men" as advisors. Not only would this device encourage support—for it was a semblance of popular government—but if matters went badly the governor could shift responsibility from his own shoulders to the nine.

Adriaen van der Donck was spokesman for the Nine as earlier he had been for the Eight Men under Kiefft. Stuyvesant felt little wisdom had been used in the elections for "each voted for one of his own stamp, thief for

The first settlement on Manhattan.

a thief, and rogue and smuggler for his brother, so that he may enjoy more vice and fraud." Although he provided for its shadow, Stuyvesant was not a devotee of the substance of democracy.

The Nine Men shortly suggested calling a genuine popular legislative assembly. Stuyvesant refused. Van der Donck was imprisoned and the governor became more intemperate than usual. In 1649, van der Donck sent a list of grievances to the States-General. In this *Remonstrance of New Amsterdam,* he complained of Stuyvesant's arbitrariness, continuing conflicts with the Indians, heavy taxes, and the lack of enough folk willing to toil in the fields. He asked for revocation of the Company charter, direct government under the States-General, and settlement of boundary problems. Van der Donck contrasted Dutch with English colonies "where neither patroons, nor lords, nor princes are known, but only the people." The States-General decreed several reforms and forgot the matter, effectively allowing the Company to thwart efforts at improvement.

Boundary problems were indeed serious. A little to the south, on the lower bank of the Delaware, was the tiny colony of New Sweden. At its height it had perhaps four hundred settlers and stretched about thirty-five miles along the river. Worried about these Swedes, Stuyvesant had Fort Casimir built in 1651 between the Swedish communities of New Elfsborg and Fort Christina. Casimir was manned by about two hundred men—almost as many as the whole population of its rival. In 1653 the Swedish governor Johan Rising, accompanied by some two hundred fifty men, attacked and captured Fort Casimir. Stuyvesant was infuriated and in the summer of 1655 sent between six hundred and seven hundred men up the Delaware to conquer the Swedes. Hopelessly outnumbered, the Swedes surrendered without firing a shot.

The colony had been tolerated as long as Sweden

Treaty with the Indians.

Landing of the Walloons.

and Holland fought as allies in the Thirty Years War. The Peace of Westphalia ended the need for sufferance and New Sweden had to be removed. The Dutch position was similar. So long as protestant England and Holland remained allied, New Netherland was tolerated. When that alliance ended, so would the Dutch colony. A preview of 1664 had occurred. Independent Swedish efforts in the New World were ended, but they had made two lasting contributions. Lutheranism, the state religion, was firmly planted in America, and the notched log cabin (itself borrowed from Finnish settlers in New Sweden) soon became a standard American home.

Stuyvesant was pleased at extending the area of his colony, but the future was bleak. Increasing boundary troubles plagued the Dutch and English colonies. In 1650, Stuyvesant negotiated, with the New England Confederation, the Treaty of Hartford. A line was drawn across Long Island southward from Oyster Bay. Lands to the east would belong to the English; to the west, the Dutch. On the mainland, English settlements would not be made within ten miles of the Hudson. The States-General ratified the treaty but the English Parliament refused to do so.

The Dutch by 1650 had built their tiny nation into the world's greatest mercantile carrier. But reasonable relations with Britain ended with the Civil War and Interregnum. The Puritans now in power realized that common religious sympathy had blinded the nation to Dutch commercial competition. England would never be able to realize the potential of its colonies so long as the Dutch, planted on the middle Atlantic coast, traded with and carried for them.

The Puritans passed the Navigation Act of 1651, and between 1652 and 1654 came the first of three Anglo-Dutch Wars (the second occurring 1664-1667, the third from 1673-1674). Pressure was never again relaxed. In

The wrath of Van Twiller.

Indians bringing tribute to the Dutch settlers.

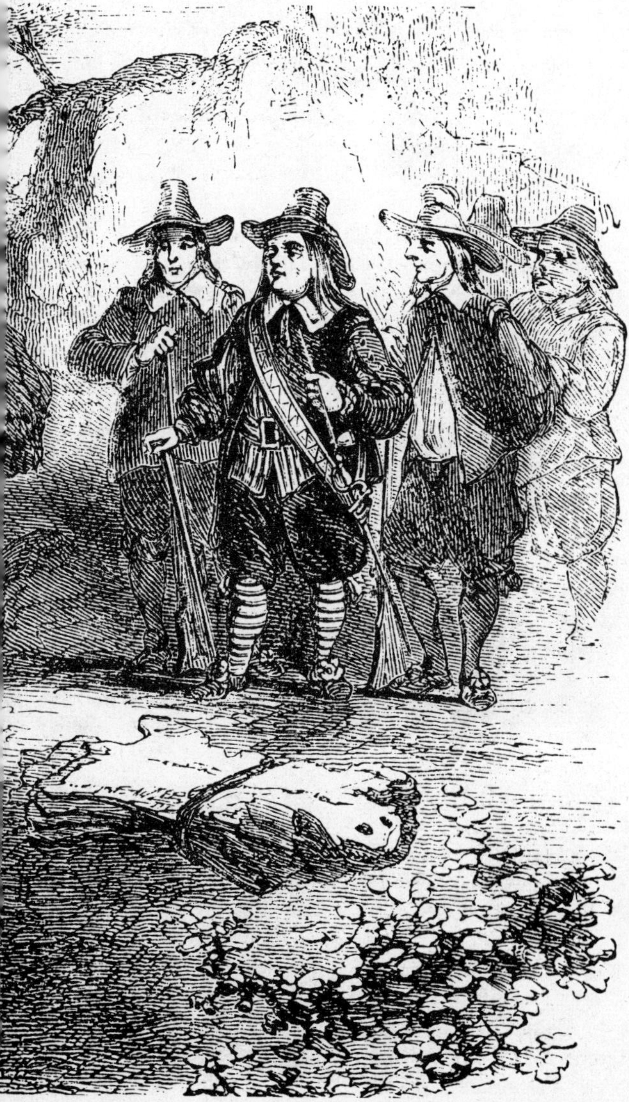

1659 Massachusetts claimed a sea-to-sea grant which cut across Dutch claims. Connecticut, following Boston's example, extended its bounds west to the Pacific in 1662. With the Stuart Restoration, Charles II continued the Puritan policy of excluding the Dutch from the colonial carrying trade. The Staple Act of 1663 followed.

Meanwhile, New Netherland had made headway in forging popular support. In 1652, in the face of mounting resentment, New Amsterdam had been allowed to form a "burgher" government. A *schout,* two *burgomeisters,* and five *schepens* ("aldermen") were chosen to form a municipal court of justice. Not popularly elected but named by Stuyvesant, it was still a step toward more limited and localized government. Other towns were soon granted the same privilege.

English pressure mounted. In 1663 Stuyvesant traveled to Boston to seek friendly settlement of conflicting claims. His journey was a failure. Upon his return, he learned that some Long Island settlements founded by the Dutch, but now predominantly English, were claiming to be under Connecticut's jurisdiction. Stuyvesant chose commissioners to find a solution. They traveled to Hartford with no more success than the Director-General had had in Boston. In 1664, Connecticut laid claim to the whole of Long Island.

That was New Netherland's fateful year. Faced by indifferent, angry, or resentful people, Stuyvesant at last instituted some semblance of popular government. A provisional assembly was formed with two men from each settlement, known as the "Twenty-Four Men." They accomplished little. Time had run out. Previous inability to participate in government had left the Dutch resentful. Those of other nationalities, irritated over Company exploitation and restrictions, were indifferent as to who owned the area. English settlers in New Netherland, envious of the greater liberties en-

The massacre of the Indians at Hoboken.

Peter Stuyvesant

joyed by their brethren to the north and south, actively hoped for a British takeover.

In 1664, Charles II granted the middle Atlantic area of the Dutch to his brother James, Duke of York and High Lord of the Admiralty. The duke appointed Colonel Richard Nicolls commander of four vessels and four hundred and fifty soldiers to sail for America to expel the Dutch. The expedition was secret so Dutch fortifications might more easily be breached if necessary.

The British fleet entered the lower harbor of New Amsterdam in August, 1664, and seized the blockhouse on Staten Island. Stuyvesant had begged the Company to furnish men and means for colonial defense. Now it was too late. The weak fort had only twenty guns, little ammunition, and few soldiers. Stuyvesant was not one to dally. As the English fleet approached, he sent his trumpeter, Anthony van Corlaer, toward the north blowing a warning for the farmers. A small, rain-swollen creek barred van Corlaer's path. The stout trumpeter swore that he would cross "in spite of the devil" himself. Unhappily, the devil seized van Corlaer's leg and pulled him under the swirling waters, but not before many farmers had heard the trumpet's shrill. Thus the ship canal which today joins the Harlem River and the Hudson received its name of Spuyten Duyvil.

Nicolls summoned Stuyvesant to surrender. The terms were liberal. The "Articles of Capitulation" allowed colonists a one and one-half year grace period in which to decide whether to leave or stay. If they remained they would enjoy the freedoms of English rule. The Council voted to inform the people of these terms. Stuyvesant disagreed, suspicious both of Nicolls and his offer. The Council insisted. Raging, Stuyvesant tore the "Articles" to shreds. He shouted that he would resist "as long as he had a leg to stand on or an arm to fight with." Few colonists were as willing to die for New Netherland as he or the late van Corlaer had been.

Stadt Huys, pillory, stocks and public well of Dutch Manhattan.

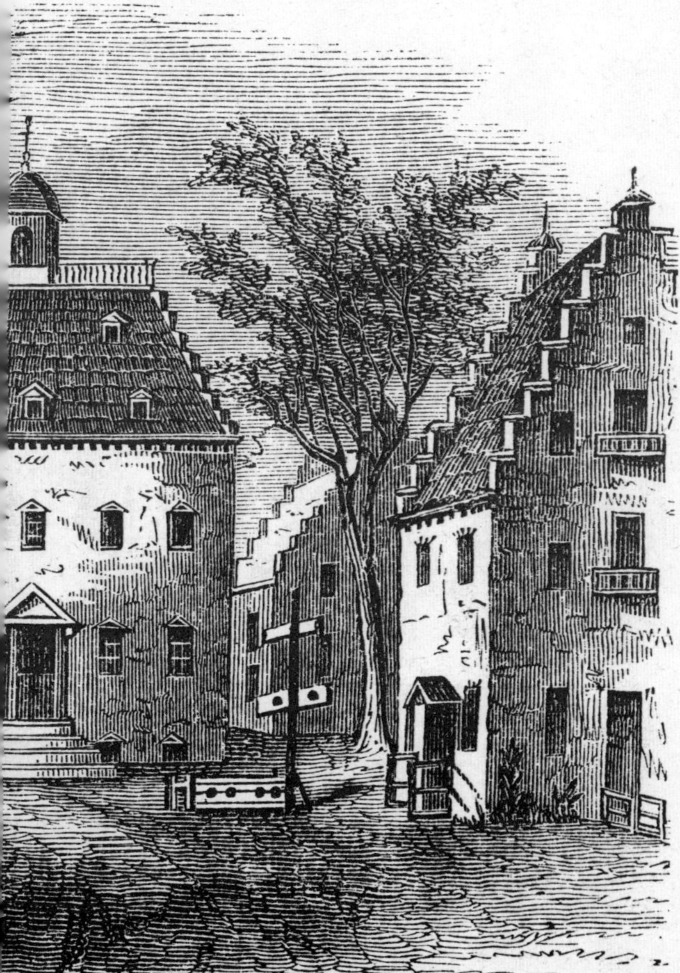

New York in 1664.

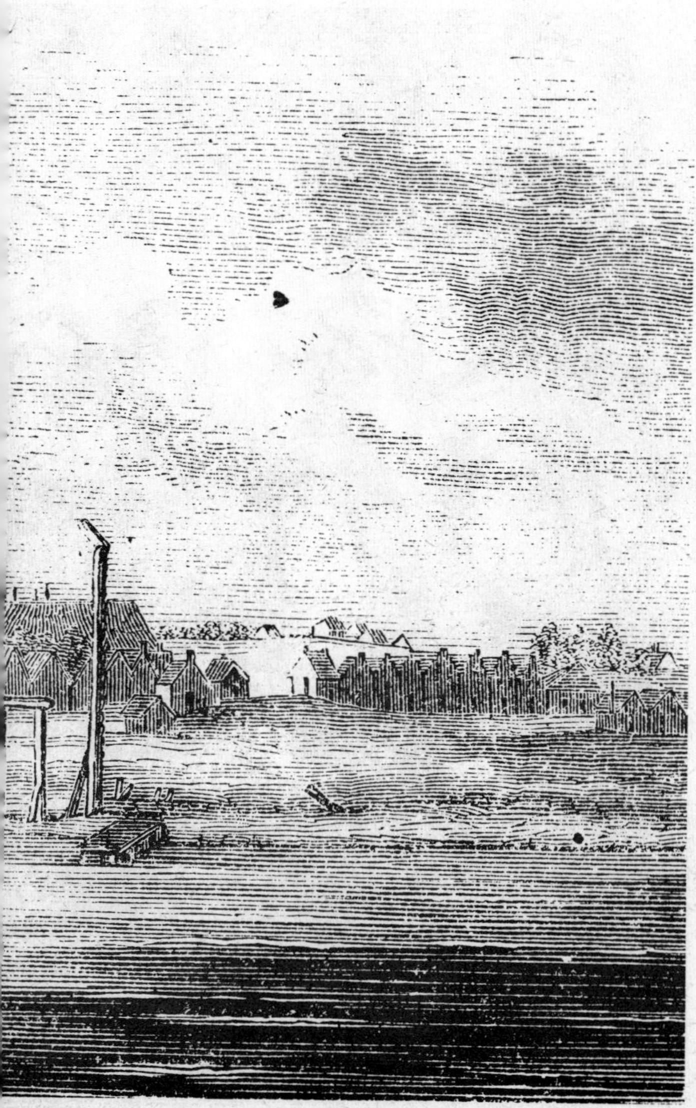

Governor Peter Stuyvesant's rage.

LOSSING-BARRITT

DUTCH COLONIAL FAILURE IN NEW YORK

They straggled to Stuyvesant's office begging him to submit. He answered repeatedly: "I would much rather be carried out dead."

Quietly and somberly the British fleet lay off the island, content to wait. As each day passed the governor's support weakened. The week following the British arrival, eighty-five principal citizens drew up a petition calling upon the governor's call for defense and signs of mutiny appeared among the too few troops. If resistance was to be made, Stuyvesant would have to fight alone. The years of mistakes now took their toll. Sadly, Pieter Stuyvesant agreed to surrender and signed the Articles of Capitulation. The British took possession of the city September 8, 1664. Not a shot had been fired

Summoned to Holland to account for his defeat, Stuyvesant completed his business there and returned to New Amsterdam—now New York—where he spent the rest of his life, busying himself with church affairs and city improvements. He even grew more sociable in the course of time. He died eight years after the surrender, about March, 1672, at the age of eighty. Could he have foreseen the future, the old soldier might have wished to live just a little longer to witness the Dutch recapture of New York during the third Anglo-Dutch War. They tenuously held the city from July 30, 1673, to November 10, 1674, before it fell once again to the British.

Dutch efforts in the New World had ended, yet these people would not—indeed could not—be forgotten. Their short-lived colony provided an abiding heritage for America. Folk legends would bring enjoyment to generations of children. Those same youngsters adopted the Easter egg and Santa Claus (St. Nicholas was the patron saint of New Amsterdam), sleighing, sledding, and ice skating. Architects centuries later still design Dutch homes to fit neatly into tiny lots in middle-class housing developments.

Stuyvesant's vain appeal. (Culver)

Place names and other Dutch terms entered the English language: the Battery, Breuckelen, Flushing, Gravesend, the Bronx, Yonkers, Haarlem, Spuyten Duyvil, Sugar Loaf, Donderberg, Wall Street, Tappen Zee, the Bouwerie, Storm King, and Anthony's Nose. Such terms as spook, scow and yacht, stoop (front porch), brief (letter), cruller and cooky, lope (to run), kill (creek), baas (boss)—these and more added to the English language's color and vitality.

Nor did the Dutch tongue pass away without a struggle. As Fort Orange became the town of Albany, the inhabitants continued to speak their native language. Over a century passed and still the Albany Dutch clung to their own speech patterns. The Constitution of 1787 had first to be translated for them before they gave their approval to it and some near Albany retained the language until near the end of the nineteenth century.

The Iroquois alliance forged by the Dutch proved valuable for their English successors. The history of North America in the struggle between the English and French might have had a much different ending had it not been for this Anglo-Indian alliance. Dutch contributions were both many and varied.

Yet men like Pieter Stuyvesant, Adriaen van der Donck, Kiliaen van Rensselaer, and others were not interested in providing cultural contributions for the English or anyone else. Interested in empire, they failed. Planted by one of the most vital European nations, blessed with an excellent location, abundant timber, good soil, fine harbors, energetic and thrifty colonists—New Netherland still perished.

Perhaps the single most important reason may be laid at the feet of the Dutch West India Company. The Provisional Order of the Company, establishing the political structure for New Netherland in 1624, was simply an unwise design of government. The office of

Director-General was a difficult one and often filled by incompetent men. The resentment they aroused must be accounted as one of the important reasons for low colonial morale. The Company's conception of New Netherland as an area primarily for exploitation was also a major weakness of the colony. Coupled with this desire for profit was the continual lack of interest in supporting the colony even when help was desperately needed.

America's abundance of free land which drew so many men to other colonies did not operate in New Netherland because of the patroon system. The crushing burden of colonial debt, a disastrous Indian war—these were other factors contributing to the eventual failure. Finally, the polyglot character of those who did come barred the development of any feeling of loyalty, patriotism, or unity among the settlers.

George Caleb Bingham's Raftsmen Playing Cards.
*Mississippi and Ohio river raftsmen were often victims
of the Harpes and other Cave-in-Rock outlaws.
(City Art Museum, St. Louis)*

MEET WILEY AND MICAJAH HARPE: UNKIND MEN

by G. G. Hatheway

Sunlight danced and sparkled on the water as Mr. Stump lounged on the bank near his cabin on the Barren River and fished. This was not the best part of Kentucky, but it could be a good place for people to settle and find a fresh start in life, and that is just what Mr. Stump was doing there in the spring of 1799. He was like ten thousand others and hundreds of thousands to follow, sturdy pioneers moving to the western fringe of civilization to take up land and hew out a farm. With luck they would live to a ripe old age in a moderate degree of comfort. Without it, at least they had tried.

It was a rough life and a lonely one for a bachelor like Stump. Pleasures and "play-parties" were rare occasions, for although this country was being settled it was yet only sparsely populated. As Mr. Stump glanced

53

up from his fishing, his eye spotted a wisp of smoke rising out of the forest some distance away on the opposite bank of the stream. Neighbors must be moving in. Stump quickly pulled in his lines and headed for his cabin. There he picked up his fiddle and a turkey he had recently shot. With fish, fiddle, turkey and with buoyant spirits he set out to greet the newcomers.

His body was discovered some time later, and his death was no accident. He had been stabbed and disemboweled, the body cavity stuffed with stones and then sunk in the river. Low water uncovered the crime, and later the confessions of a dying man solved it. Mr. Stump had died at the hands of Wiley and Micajah Harpe.

The setting for the sanguine career of the peripatetic Harpe brothers extended across the present states of Tennessee, Kentucky, southern Illinois, and down into Mississippi. There, during the years from 1795 to 1804, Wiley and Micajah Harpe carved out a reputation that for unadulterated brutality had no equal, one that included between 30 and 40 murders. Some accounts place the number as high as 58, but we can never know the true figure for the brothers themselves lost count. It was a career that sprang from the conditions of life in the United States in the backwash of the Revolutionary War and, particularly, of life as it existed on the westward-moving fringe of settlement where "tough" qualities in men and women were often necessary for simple survival.

The Harpe boys, Micajah born about 1768 and Wiley some two years later, were native North Carolinians. Of their early years records are maddeningly silent. Apparently there was little to distinguish the Harpe family from the rest of backwoods North Carolina folk until the former English colonies declared themselves to be free and independent. Then, when his sons were about eight and six years old respectively, Father Harpe decided to remain a true and loyal subject

MEET WILEY AND MICAJAH HARPE

of His Majesty King George III. And when the American Revolution made a fiery thrust deep into the back country, he fought on the Loyalist side with Major Patrick Ferguson at the battle of King's Mountain.

The American Revolution, like almost any civil war, left deep and long-lasting wounds. Those who supported the losing side, or even those who remained neutral, were persecuted long after open hostilities had ceased. Many Loyalists had fled the country during the course of the Revolution and even more after the return of peace. Some went to the Floridas and the British West Indies, thousands more went north into Canada and Nova Scotia, while a few returned to England. But many, probably most, of the Loyalists found that moving away was beyond their means and so they returned to their homes and farms to settle down again, trying to take up where they had left off their work.

Father Harpe was a member of this group. Supposedly protected from persecution under the 5th and 6th articles of the treaty of peace between Great Britain and the United States, these returning Tories found themselves open to discrimination and persecution of a subtle and sometimes a flagrant nature. So it was that Micajah and Wiley Harpe, aged about 15 and 13 respectively when peace came in 1783, grew up in an atmosphere of hatred—at least they later claimed this was true.

Until 1795 their lives are shrouded as far as the records show, but in that year the present state of Tennessee played host to a band of four pioneers and the trail of violence began. One of the group, Micajah Harpe, measured six feet three inches in his bare feet. His large, fleshy face frowned out from beneath a coarse mat of black, curly hair. Twenty-seven years old, he was in the prime of manhood with a straight and powerful build; large-boned, broad-chested, and equipped with a sullen temper, he was the dominant

55

member of the group. His brother Wiley, considerably smaller, likewise sported a mat of hair, but it was straighter and of a reddish cast. His feral face wore a "downcast" expression most of the time.

Romance had entered the life of Micajah and he had two "wives" to prove it. These were the sisters named Susan, or Susanna, and Betsey Roberts. Susan, the woman who steadfastly maintained that she was legally married to Micajah, is reputed to have been tall, rawboned, homely, and in her middle twenties. Sister Betsey, the auxiliary wife, had light hair, blue eyes, and was rather pretty. Wiley was not married, but the brothers undoubtedly shared all their possessions.

For about two years this "family" wandered around eastern Tennessee in company with a band of renegade Creek and Cherokee Indians eking out a living by raiding small farms, stealing what was movable and burning the rest. But the two brothers and wives wearied of the life, and the bitterly cold winter of 1796-97 figured largely in their determination to settle down. So Big and Little Harpe and the ladies built a cabin on Beaver Creek in the rolling country about eight miles west of Knoxville.

Located strategically at the junction of the three roads that tapped the back country of Virginia, North Carolina, and South Carolina, Knoxville throve on the heavy annual tourist trade of thousands of westering pioneers. At the time of the Harpes' arrival it had less than a 500 permanent population, but traffic between Knoxville and Nashville, 197 miles farther west, was so heavy that immigrants reportedly crowded each other from the road. In the summer of 1795 some 26,000 people crossed the Cumberland River in two months.

While the Harpes had been wandering with their Indian associates, Tennessee became a state in the Union on June 1, 1796. Knoxville, growing rapidly, filled with strangers both domestic and foreign. With the influx of

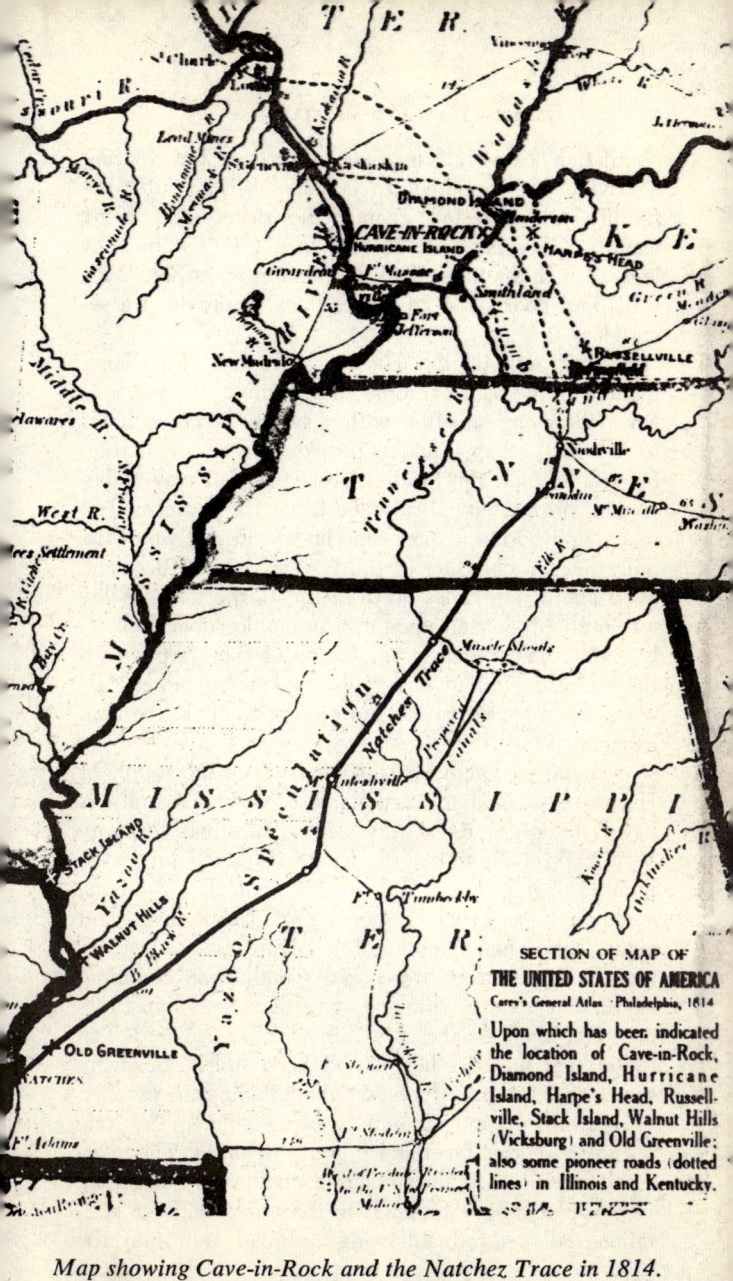

SECTION OF MAP OF
THE UNITED STATES OF AMERICA
Carey's General Atlas - Philadelphia, 1814

Upon which has been indicated the location of Cave-in-Rock, Diamond Island, Hurricane Island, Harpe's Head, Russellville, Stack Island, Walnut Hills (Vicksburg) and Old Greenville; also some pioneer roads (dotted lines) in Illinois and Kentucky.

Map showing Cave-in-Rock and the Natchez Trace in 1814.

population came an increase of crime, but roaring Knoxville was prepared. In January of 1793, after the sheriff had protested against the rickety old Knox County jail, a new jail 16 feet on a side was built of logs 12 inches square, laid double and crosswise. With walls and floor some 24 inches thick, it provided a secure lock-up.

Having settled, the Harpes cleared a little land, planted some small crops, and visited the mart at Knoxville every so often with a supply of cured hams to sell. Harpe hams quickly developed a fine reputation for quality, and the brothers were in a fair way of becoming prosperous. Meanwhile Little Harpe decided to marry and within a short time he wooed and won Miss Sally Rice, a daughter of the Reverend John Rice who lived about four miles north of the Harpe farm. Wiley was probably looked upon as a desirable, albeit unlovely, catch. The previous association of the Harpes with the renegade Indian raiders was unknown; rather they were recognized as successful entrepreneurs in the ham business.

Demand was high for Harpe hams, but the supply of Harpe pigs failed to keep pace. Secretly the brothers began to appropriate stray hogs. The great disparity between the number of hams marketed and the number of hogs raised was not lost upon the neighbors, among whom it was rumored that Harpe hogs had eight legs. There were additional unsettling developments. The brothers were seen spending an abnormal amount of time in drinking, gambling, and horse racing, and then in the late fall of 1798 Edward Tiel found that his best horses had been stolen. Believing the Harpes to be guilty, he set about finding the proof.

Enlisting the aid of some of his neighbors, Tiel rode out to the Harpe farm and found it deserted. The unofficial posse did discover where a number of horses had very recently been tethered to trees, and without hesitation galloped off following a broad trail into the

MEET WILEY AND MICAJAH HARPE

Cumberland mountains. They had not gone far before they discovered exactly what they expected—the Harpe brothers with Edward Tiel's horses in tow. No resistance was offered. The Harpes surrendered meekly and the party turned back in the direction of Knoxville and its thick-walled jail.

The deficiencies of the posse were made apparent in a short time. Probably the very meekness of the Harpes' surrender had disarmed their captors and proper vigilance was not observed. The Harpes easily sized up the situation and about five miles from Knoxville they dove into a patch of tangled underbrush, escaping with hardly a scratch. Nettled at their brush with frontier law the brothers went to soak their heated tempers at Hughes' Rowdy Groggery, a roadside tavern located a short distance from their farm. They finished off an evening of drinking by murdering a total stranger. When the body was found it was reported to have been disemboweled, the body filled with stones and sunk in the Holston River. This was a particular Harpe trademark, apparently learned from their former Indian partners in crime.

Undoubtedly before they left their cabin with Tiel's horses they gave instructions to their wives to meet them near Cumberland Gap. It was about sixty wintry miles by a rough trail from Knoxville to the Gap, but there in December of 1798 the group reassembled. Then, staying fairly close to the Wilderness Road, they drifted into Kentucky.

The Wilderness Road was then one of the main-traveled land routes to the west, and virtually the only route from Virginia and North Carolina into the "Kaintuck" country. From Cumberland Gap the road stretched northwest through Pineville and London to Hazel Patch. There the road forked; the right fork headed north to Boonsborough and Judge Richard Henderson's lands near Winchester and Lexington, the

1833 view (false to the actual scene) of Cave-in-Rock from a Charles Bodmer drawing.

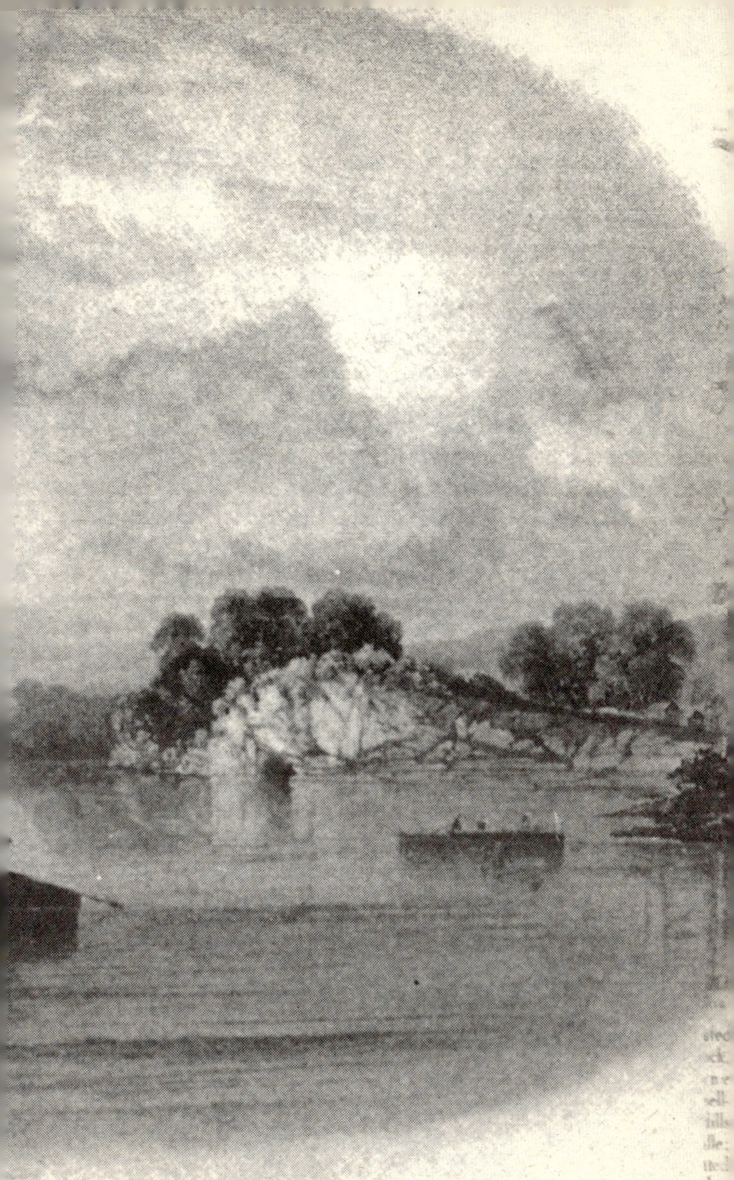

*Interior of Cave-in-Rock about 1825.
From a C. A. Lesueur drawing.*

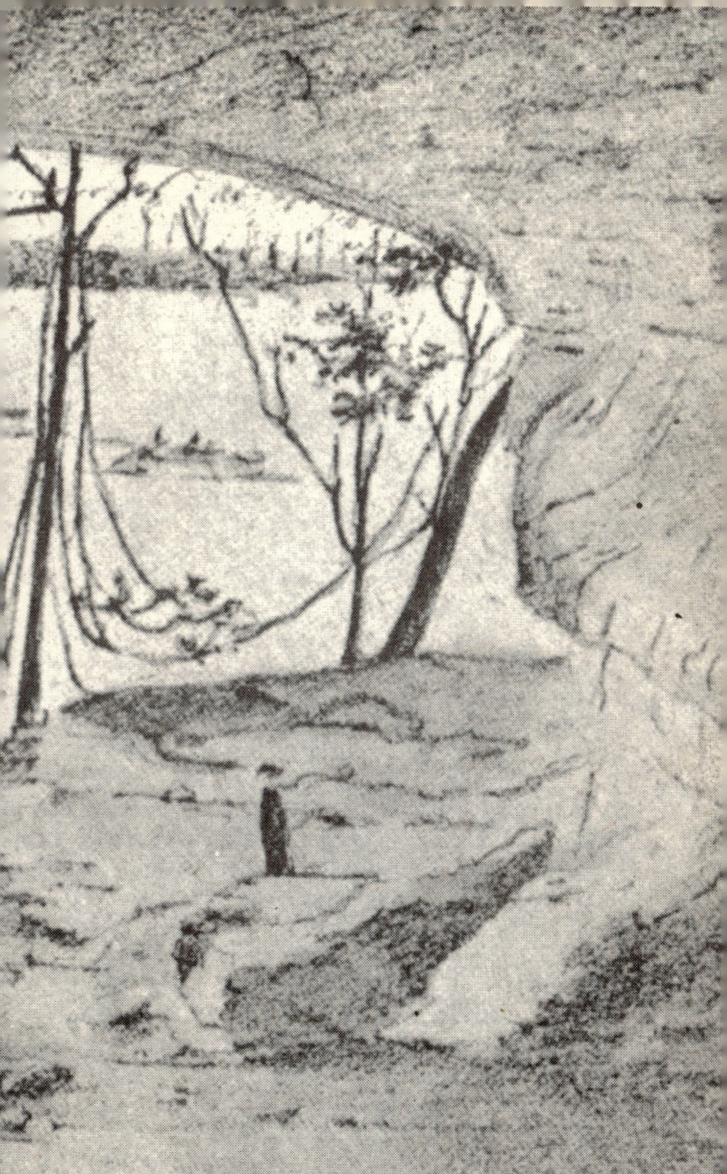

left fork continued northwest to Crab Orchard, St. Asaph's station, Harrodsburg, Bradstown, and Louisville.

In the 1770's and 1780's this Wilderness Road was the scene of scores of murders committed by wandering bands of irreconcilable Indians who took that method of protesting the loss of their lands to the onrushing settlers. By the mid 1790's the Indian menace had abated, but the Wilderness Road continued to bear the reputation of a dangerous highway, for in addition to natural hazards, dozens of bandits preyed on the unwary traveler. Such a route as the Wilderness Road, with Cumberland Gap a funnel through which must pass travelers on business, peddlers, land buyers, and others carrying sums of money, attracted those bent upon easy gain.

On their way from Cumberland Gap to the forks at Hazel Patch the new road agents, the Harpes, killed a peddler named Peyton and two other people traveling west from Maryland to take up land. These murders kept the brothers and their wives in pin money and clothing. Early on the morning of December 12, 1798, they arrived at John Farris' Inn, some distance east of Crab Orchard, and met Stephen Langford, a young Virginian on his way to visit a kinsman who lived in Crab Orchard. The guileless Langford invited the group to breakfast with him and the Harpes readily agreed. He explained to them that he was worried about the next stretch of road he must travel. It bore a particularly evil reputation, and he felt it would be safer for all if they traveled together.

The Harpes looked stout enough to suit him. He invited their aid and company and they consented. The presence of the three women probably accounts for Langford's faith in these total strangers; with women in the group, he felt they were honest. Moreover all three ladies were rather obviously in a family condition; they

MEET WILEY AND MICAJAH HARPE

just had to be simple travelers. Breakfast finished they went to their horses and shortly after with a cheery wave they all set off up the trail.

Sometime later Langford's body was discovered behind a log at the side of the road. No real attempt had been made to conceal it. He had been shot squarely in the center of the back. Cattle drovers who made the gory discovery were headed in the direction of Farris' Inn, and the body was carried there where it was readily identified. A posse was formed and set off in search of the Harpes, the only persons known to have been last in company with Langford. The entire party was captured on Christmas Day of 1798 just shivering forlornly on a log in the forest. Once again the Harpes gave up without a struggle and were taken to Stanford, Kentucky, for a hearing before the Court of Quarter Sessions.

Christmas season passed and the Harpes were brought before the court on January 4, 1799. A parade of witnesses made positive identification of the body of Langford after its exhumation. Among others, Farris' daughter-in-law testified that the Harpes and Langford had set off together on the morning of the murder. Captain Joseph Ballenger, a Stanford, Kentucky, merchant and leader of the capturing posse, testified that he had found a number of Langford's personal articles in possession of the Harpes when they were apprehended on their log in the woods. This was a preliminary hearing, and the court took little time to decide that the entire company of Harpe men and women should be made to appear before the District Court of Danville, Kentucky, at the April term to stand trial for the murder of Stephen Langford. The next day they were moved from Stanford to the jail in Danville under armed guard.

Once again we must account for the ease with which the Harpes were captured, for they would not always be this tractable. The answer must lie in the fact that each of the Harpe women was pregnant. They needed to get in somewhere warm, and a stout jail was infinitely better than a log in the wintry woods if one was about to deliver. Moreover, in jail the medical expenses would be at the cost of the local government. So it was that during their extended stay at the Danville lock-up each of the three wives gave birth. The jailer was kept busy hustling hyson tea, meals, and midwives into and out of the cells.

Early in February Betsey was delivered of a fine boy to be named Joe. Exactly one month later her sister Susan presented a daughter, Lovey, to the world. Just one month after that, Sally Rice Harpe was also delivered of a girl. A fascinating feature of this last confinement was that in addition to the usual amount of tea and sugar, Sally consumed one quart of whiskey which cost the jailer 1s 6d., but there was no expenditure made for a midwife.

Meanwhile security at the jail was tightened. The jailer's account book records the purchase of a new lock for the front door, two horse locks to chain Wiley and Micajah, and three pounds of nails for a general strengthening of the building. All the Harpes enjoyed their rest, their regular meals, and watched the repairs on the jail with a certain detached interest. The men had no idea of submitting to the trial. They stayed on through the winter—January, February, and the first two weeks in March. Then on the sixteenth of that month Wiley and Micajah Harpe left by going straight through the jail wall. An item in the jailer's accounts reads, "mending the wall in jail where the prisoners escaped . . . 12s."

In leaving their wives behind to face trial neither Wiley nor Micajah appears to have feared the outcome. Perhaps they knew already what frontier justice would produce. At the first round of trials Susan Roberts (or

Harpe) was found "guilty." The very next day, April 18, Micajah's auxiliary wife Betsey, who now gave her name as Elizabeth Walker, was tried on the same evidence and found "not guilty." Sally, who also took the alias "Roberts," was next up before the court and was acquitted. Then Susan obtained a retrial and the case against the Harpe women was closed when a *nolle prosequi* was entered in the records.

The jury of peers was tender toward frontier women, young motherhood, and a plea of repentance. Following the trial the good people of Danville, certain from the testimony that Susan, Betsey, and Sally had reformed, outdid charity in helping the girls to start life afresh. Along with a collection of clothes and money, they gave the rescued sinners an old mare and set them on the long road to Knoxville, Tennessee. The three young mothers traveled about thirty miles before they came to the Green River. There they swapped the horse for a canoe, piled in, and happily paddled off downriver to find their mates. The devotion of these women for their men is nowhere more apparent.

Meanwhile Wiley and Micajah had been active. Immediately after their escape from the Danville jail a general order was sent to all sheriffs and constables notifying them of the escape and requesting their assistance and vigilance. Then in April the Governor of Kentucky, James Garrard, authorized Captain Joseph Ballenger to organize another posse and sweep the northern portion of the state clear of criminals. Ballenger was actually a jump ahead of the governor, for the captain and his men had already taken the trail of the Harpes and quickly cornered them near the headwaters of the Rolling Fork River.

This time there were no encumbrances; there was no "family way" to contend with, and Ballenger's posse met a hot reception. The Harpes boldly shot it out with them and escaped into a dense canebrake under cover

MEET WILEY AND MICAJAH HARPE

of darkness. The posse was skilled in tracking, but lacking in courage, and although Henry Scaggs, an old Revolutionary War veteran and member of the posse, stoutly urged them to push on and capture the Harpes in the canes, the chase was abandoned.

Wiley and Micajah then swung in a wide loop heading south and west, killing as they traveled. A thirteen-year-old boy, John Trabue, was waylaid and killed for a bag of flour he was carrying. An ironic twist of fate placed old Henry Scaggs, the war veteran, at the home of Daniel Trabue, John's father, at the very time of the murder. They were discussing the raising of a posse to pursue the Harpes. On learning of the murder of young John, Trabue and Scaggs posted a $300 reward notice in the Frankfort *Palladium* for the capture of the Harpes.

Before that notice was off the press the Harpes had killed a man by the name of Dooley in Metcalfe County and then Mr. Stump about eight miles below Bowling Green on the Barren River. After disposing of Stump's body the two brothers continued down the Barren River to its junction with the Green River. There they rejoined their wives, whom we left paddling down the Green, and together once again the entire group went down the Green River to the Ohio River and then to an infamous place called Cave-In-Rock.

Cave-In-Rock, in what is now Hardin County, Illinois, is situated on the north bank of the Ohio River at the base of a high bluff. About fifty feet wide at the mouth, the cave only extends about 160 feet back into the bluff. At the rear of the cave is a nearly circular chamber about 60 feet in diameter with a smaller "room" off at the right-hand side. It had long been imagined by the Indians to be the abode of a manitou (or spirit) whom they held in awe. An unsavory man named Samuel Mason, bringing his family down the

Ohio River, obtained a shadowy title to the cave and established there in the 1790's a business that he called "Liquor Vault and House of Entertainment." Now inhabited by "spirits" for sure, this emporium became a favorite resort of rowdies and the infamous Ohio River pirates.

These inland, but waterborne, pirates preyed on the increasing traffic carried by the Ohio and Mississippi system. Each year in the navigation season hundreds of boats, most of them flatboats, would pass down the Ohio. Some carried westering families, others the produce of those people already settled in the upper Ohio valley. The methods employed by the river pirates varied, but usually involved luring a boat within range of an ambush and slaughtering the occupants of the craft. The boat and its stores would then be appropriated by the pirates. They could take over the task of piloting it on to New Orleans, there to sell the goods, or they might sell the goods to following pioneers. Experienced flatboaters and keelboatmen were not usually caught in this type of trap, but hundreds of families who had never heard of Cave-In-Rock floated down the beautiful Ohio and into the clutches of the pirates who infested both banks of the river from the "Liquor Vault" to Fort Massac.

Shortly after the murder of young John Trabue, a second posse was formed under the leadership of a Captain Young. Commissioned to seize all criminals lurking on the Kentucky shore of the Ohio River, Young's posse, sweeping northward to the Ohio from the central part of Kentucky, was not very successful in making captures but it did succeed in pushing a large number of case-hardened toughs out of Kentucky and into the territory north of the river. Just ahead of Young's posse the five grown Harpes and their three little ones made it to Cave-In-Rock at about the height of the spring season on flatboaters.

For a brief time this new family in the pirate band

J. B. Alberts' 1916 drawing showing the interior of Cave-in-Rock and entrance to the upper cave.

J. B. Alberts

rubbed along with the older resident group. But friction almost inevitably produced heated disagreement, and the way in which it occurred points out a difference between the Harpes and the pirates. On a particularly successful day two flatboats of westward bound families had been ambushed. In the fight most of these luckless persons were killed, only two or three survivors being brought ashore. A bonfire was built near the mouth of the cave and the pirates prepared to divide up the loot.

During the excitement of the celebration one of the survivors, a young man, was seized by Wiley and Micajah. The two brothers also quietly took one of the horses acquired in the day's operations and led their charges to the top of the bluff. There, overlooking the pirates' bonfire, they stripped the man, tied him to the horse, and then drove the two over the cliff into the bonfire to their death. This was an act of needless brutality—not that the pirates regretted the killing of the man so much as the fact they were incensed at the sacrifice of a valuable horse. The pirates of Cave-In-Rock sent the Harpes packing.

From the Ohio River they traveled and murdered southward and eastward into Tennessee and then back again into western Kentucky. Newspapers were full of the facts and figures as the Harpes continued to carve out their career. Rich and poor, young and old, Negro and white, none was safe from attack. Again posses were formed for the pursuit and apprehension of the killers, and one of these succeeded in chasing the brothers and their wives very closely in Kentucky. The fleeing band came to a clearing near what was known as Duncan's Bridge on the Mud River. There they were forced to stop to water the horses.

As they stood in a small clearing by a spring near the edge of the stream one of the children began to cry. Swearing that the crying would lead to the capture of the entire group, Big Harpe ordered the mother to make the child stop, but the crying continued. He flew into a rage, shambled over to Sally, the terrified mother, snatched the baby from her arms, and taking the infant by the heels smashed its brains out against a tree. This done he flung the pitiful body out into the brush. When at death's doorstep a few months later, Big Harpe confessed that this was the sole murder he regretted.

Not long after this in the late summer of 1799, the Harpes arrived at the home of Moses Stegall, near Dixon, in the hilly country of western Kentucky. Stegall was not at home, but William Love, a surveyor who did business with Stegall, was there along with Stegall's wife and infant son of about four months. According to a traditional story the whole group supped together and shortly afterward retired for the night, with the Harpes and William Love sharing the cabin loft. Love was soon dispatched by splitting his skull with an axe. The reason often cited was that Love snored too loudly for the comfort of the Harpes. With the annoyance removed, the group settled down to a restful night.

Early in the morning they awakened and breakfast preparations began. Mrs. Stegall went about her work with the pots and pans while Wiley and Micajah gently rocked the baby in the corner of the room. As the meal was being served Mrs. Stegall made a remark that the men certainly were good fathers; the baby had not cried once. She leaned over the cradle in motherly fashion to admire her child and then discovered the terrible reason for the silence; the baby's throat had been slashed from ear to ear.

The brothers put the hysterical mother to death as well, finished their breakfast, set fire to the cabin, and rode off. Moses Stegall returned shortly after this to find the charred remains of the latest victims of the

MEET WILEY AND MICAJAH HARPE

Harpes. Apparently there were enough tracks and signs around for Stegall to deduce that the affair was no accident and, though he did not know who had last been at his home, he organized the inevitable posse to set out to find them.

By nightfall the avengers had located the route taken by the Harpes and had been trailing them for several miles. Darkness put a temporary end to pursuit but with the dawn they set out again from a camp on the Pond River. Within about an hour the posse found two dead dogs on the trail, and a short search disclosed the bodies of two men, the bodies still warm. The chase pressed on, and it was not long before the quarry was sighted on a distant hillside. The Harpes spotted their followers at about the same moment. Big Harpe flung himself into the saddle and rode off with his two wives. Little Harpe abandoned his wife and sped off into the brush on foot.

The posse spread out and soon located Little Harpe's wife. She told her captors the direction Big Harpe had taken and then resigned herself to her fate. The leaders of the posse raced on. Within two miles Big Harpe and his wives were spotted. The killer abandoned the women to the posse and spurred his horse onward.

Stegall and a man named Lieper, now in the lead as the chase thundered along the trail, steadily closed the distance. Drawing within range they began to shoot, and at the second or third shot Harpe was hit in the leg. Immediately he drew rein, swung around and attempted to shoot down Lieper who was a bit ahead. Lieper was the quicker shot and his bullet caught Harpe near the spine as he was turning. As Lieper pulled abreast of him Harpe drew a tomahawk and attempted to split the man's head. In the scuffle Harpe shook off the two men and flogged his horse into a dead run once again. But the killer's horse was jaded, and he, twice wounded. Within half a mile Lieper and Mathew Christy managed to close in and pull Big

Harpe out of the saddle. He fell heavily in the trail, unable to move, glaring at his captors.

As the rest of the party rode up and drew rein they could see that Harpe was dying. Someone fetched some water from a nearby spring, and then under questioning Harpe began to confess to his crimes. An enraged Stegall took out a pocket knife and announced his intention of cutting off Harpe's head, but he was dissuaded and the dying man rambled on with his tale of violence. After about an hour it became obvious that the end was very near. Harpe had lost a great deal of blood and his speech was now faltering.

Stegall approached again and pointed a gun at Harpe who weakly moved his head from side to side to avoid the shot, clinging to the last shred of time. Stegall then muttered something about keeping the head for a trophy and shot Harpe in the side. A traditional version of the scene has it that even this shot did not kill Harpe outright, and as Stegall went about cutting off the head Harpe ground out between his clenched teeth that Stegall's knife was dull and Stegall was a damned poor butcher. At last the gory business was finished. The head was wrapped up and stuffed into Squire Silas McBee's saddlebags. The rest of the body was left in the woods for the wild animals, and the posse turned back to Dixon with their trophy and captives.

On the return trip the heat of the late summer's day worked its way on the grisly object in McBee's saddlebags, so four and a half miles north of the town of Dixon the group stopped to make a display. At the crossroads they pruned and sharpened the top of a sapling and impaled the head on its point. Today, near that spot a rough brownstone marker about three feet high bears the crudely carved letters "H H" and the place is still known locally as Harpe's Head.

The three Harpe women were arraigned before the

Court of Quarter Sessions of Henderson County on September 4, 1799, and were bound over to stand trial for the murder of Mary Stegall, her son James Stegall, and Mr. William Love. On October 29th and 30th the trials were held before a packed courtroom. Apparently the evidence against the three women was completely circumstantial and the court did not recognize the status of "accomplice." All three were found "not guilty" and were released from custody.

This time, however, the ladies did not go back to their old habits. With the exception of Susan, Big Harpe's legal wife, they remarried. Betsey moved to Tennessee and Sally Rice Harpe, the minister's daughter, at last was saved from sin, married, a second time (bigamously), and moved to Illinois Territory. There remained one score to settle—Wiley.

Following the death of his brother, Wiley assumed various aliases and under the name of John Setton he joined a gang that operated along the Natchez Trace. The system of commerce then in use on the great interior river system of the United States consisted for the most part of trips downriver by flatboat and return journeys by land. The flatboat might be constructed, for example, at Cincinnati, Ohio. There it would be laden with pigs, flour, potash, honey, barrels of apples, and so forth. Then it would be floated down the Ohio and the Mississippi perhaps to New Orleans where the cargo and flatboat would be sold—the cargo for consumption or for reshipment, the flatboat to be broken up for lumber or for firewood.

The farmer or flatboatman with cash in his pockets then would trudge up the trails along the east bank of the great river to Natchez where he would take the famous "Trace" to Nashville and thence back to his home near Cincinnati. The Natchez Trace was a great land link between the producing region in the Ohio valley and the markets at New Orleans, acting as a major artery of trade. It was not really a good road, but it was about the only road, and historically roads that stimulate travel have also stimulated the base acquisitive instincts of men.

On the American frontier, during the interim between the retrocession of Louisiana to France in October of 1800 and the assumption of regular control by United States troops in December of 1803, the sinews of the arm of the law withered terribly. A criminal element in New Orleans, present almost since its founding, had never really been conquered. Now in that city and in other river towns on both sides of the international boundary the unsettled conditions of political authority, the increasing river and land commerce, and the vulnerability of the traveler all favored the illicit activities of bandit gangs.

Wiley Harpe had rejoined forces with the Samuel Mason gang now operating along the Natchez Trace, having given up at Cave-In-Rock, and for several years with lookouts at inns, taverns, and houses of ill-fame to spot likely victims the gang thrived. Several attempts to capture them misfired. In 1802 Governor Claiborne of the Mississippi Territory offered a $2000 reward for the capture of Mason, the gang leader, and Wiley Harpe. He directed Colonel Daniel Burnet to form a posse of 15 or 20 picked men to scour the woods from New Orleans to the Yazoo River. He also solicited the aid of United States troops in the search.

Apparently such a concerted effort drove the gang across the Mississippi into Spanish-French territory, for they were reported captured by Spanish authorities and taken to New Madrid, in what is now southeastern Missouri. In the investigations Mason attempted to throw all the blame for a large number of robberies and killings onto Harpe, and the latter blamed Mason for everything. The gang had committed no crime in territory under Spanish jurisdiction so the authorities decided to send them to New Orleans, where they

1917 photograph of Cave-in-Rock.

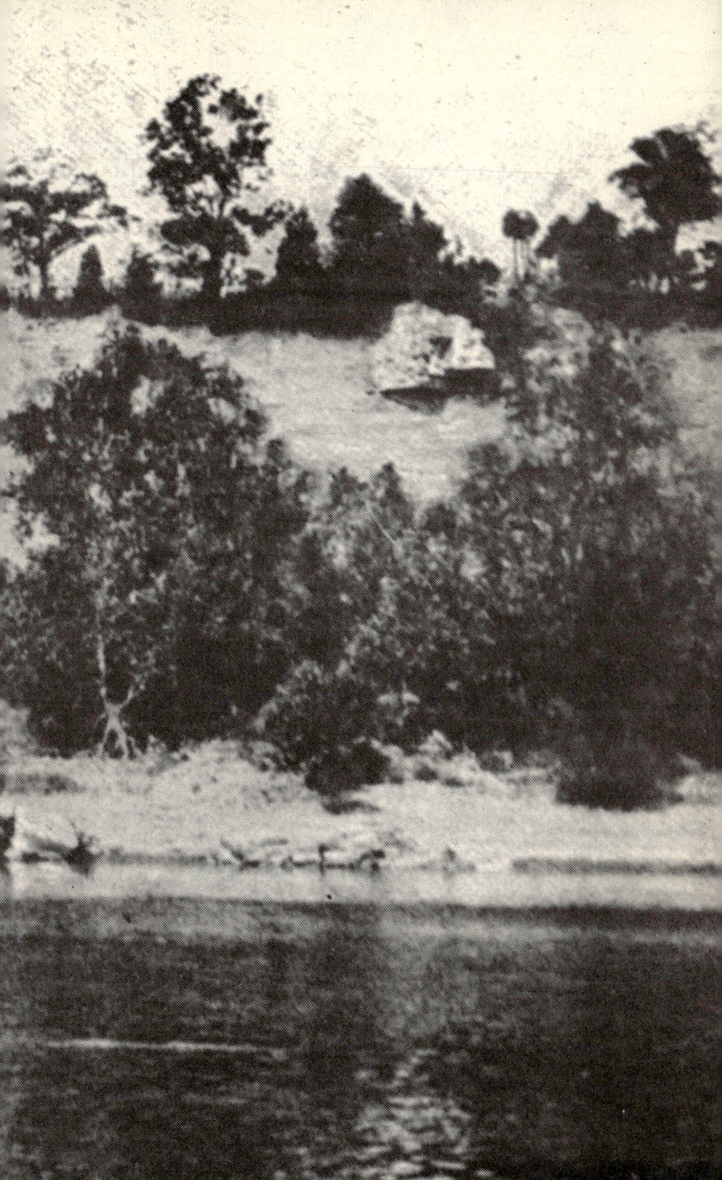

could be turned over to American authorities. Near Natchez the gang overwhelmed their guards and broke away.

A tangled series of appearances and disappearances of both Mason and Harpe followed, but the confidence of Wiley Harpe in his leader had run out. In January of 1804 Harpe and an accomplice named May murdered Samuel Mason, cut off his head, wrapped it in clay, and shortly after appeared at Washington, Mississippi, seat of the territorial government, to collect the reward. There was some difficulty in obtaining positive identification, and while Harpe and May were cooling their heels someone took a closer look at these frontier "heroes." A trap was laid, and when the two appeared to collect the reward money they were seized without a fight.

Soon a notice was posted at Natchez landing asking for the positive identification of Harpe, alias Setton, and a steady stream of boatmen offered their services. John Bowman and others identified various scars and bodily features, and Wiley Harpe was bound over to stand trial. Wiley seemed to have given up running and resigned himself to execution. He had no defense at all, and before the Circuit Court at Greenville, Mississippi, he was found guilty. The records of the court carry this dry entry, dated February 4, 1804:

> John Setton who has been found guilty of robbery at the present term was this day set to the bar and the sentence of the court pronounced upon him as follows, that on Wednesday the eighth day of the present month he be taken to the place of execution and there to be hung up by the neck, between the hours of ten o'clock in the forenoon and four in the afternoon, until he is dead, dead, dead.

LEXINGTON, *Sept.* 10.

The two murderers by the name of Harps, who killed Mr. Langford last winter in the wilderness, and were arrested and broke the Danville goal, killed a family on Pond river, by the name of Staple on the 22d day of August, and burnt the house; a party of men pursued and overtook them and their women; the Harps parted. Micajah Harp, took two of the women off with him; the men pursued him, and in riding about 10 or 12 miles, caught him, having previously shot him. He confessed the killing of Mr. Stump on Big Barren; he also confessed of their killing 17 or 18 besides; they killed two men near Robertson's Lick, the day before they burnt Staple's house. They had with them eight horses and a considerable quantity of plunder, seven pair of saddle bags, &c. They cut off his head. The women were taken to the Red banks. The above took place on Pond river in the county of Muhlenburg.

Facsimile of a news item regarding the capture of Micajah Harpe dated September 10, 1799.

MEET WILEY AND MICAJAH HARPE

On a chilly Wednesday in 1804 Wiley Harpe, alias John Setton, twirled in the gentle breeze, gave up his ghost, and travelers on Natchez Trace were a little bit safer. The gangs were by no means snuffed out; crime continued to march on in the frontier environment. It was just that one of the more vicious practitioners was no longer on the scene.

The old town of Greenville, Mississippi, has disappeared with time, and today a gravel road runs between tilled fields where the town once stood. People who lived around there can still recall vividly the stories handed down through four generations and can direct one to the site of the gallows field or to the place where Wiley Harpe's head was displayed on a pole at the north edge of town. For that was his fate as it had been the fate of his brother.

The story of the Harpes is a tale of a long and seemingly senseless string of murders, but is more than that. It illustrates a paradox of this frontier, for although Tennessee could be a fertile land and the famed bluegrass country of Kentucky was almost without parallel, the shadow of the serpent lay across the land. In this land of promise where a man really could make a fresh start in life, a disturbing undercurrent of violence lay just beneath the surface ready to bubble forth like a poisoned spring.

Lest the picture be distorted, it must be emphasized that the Harpes were not alone in crime. There were many other misfits on that same frontier. There were the renegade band of Indians cast out by their own people, the river pirates based at Cave-In-Rock, the highwaymen on the Natchez Trace, and there were many others operating singly or in groups. The Harpes were simply outstandingly pitiless members of this class of citizens.

Ironically they missed the opportunity to become folk heroes in buckskin. Consider the careers of Simon

MEET WILEY AND MICAJAH HARPE

Kenton, Anthony Wayne, or William Henry Harrison. Although these men employed deceit and treachery, ferocity and terror, their deeds won them admiration because they were perpetrated against the "common enemy." They could whet the knife edge of their tempers on the tough, copper-colored skin of the Indian. Had the Harpes employed their own ample skills in the killing of Indians rather than white men, their "score" would have made them folk heroes of a far more gigantic stature than Daniel Boone or Davy Crockett. But when their father made that fateful decision to support his king during the Revolution, the die was cast.

In the patriot persecution of Loyalists, the seeds of hatred were sown to strike deep roots in the minds of two young boys. In addition to whatever other lessons they learned, whatever skills they developed as frontiersmen, Wiley and Micajah Harpe carried an abiding bitterness with them over the mountains into that agrarian Eden. There, with conditions favoring equally the life of virtue or the life of crime, they enjoyed the freedom to wreak vengeance on whom they chose.

Benjamin West

BENJAMIN WEST: THE QUAKER REMBRANDT

by Robert Hardy Andrews

William Penn who founded Pennsylvania as a refuge for Quakers fleeing persecution in England had been dead 20 years, and Thomas, one of his four sons, ruled the colony as hereditary proprietor when Benjamin West was born, upstairs over a roadside tavern in Springfield Township near Philadelphia, October 10, 1738. Thomas Penn's sons, John and Richard, continued the dynasty, taking their turns as lieutenant-governor. They were fugitives from the American Revolution, back in the mother country to stay, when they first heard of Benjamin West. By then the youngest of an impecunious Quaker innkeeper's 10 children had conquered England, with no weapon but a paintbrush. The first American artist to go abroad, at a time when even Benjamin Franklin found it prudent to leave London and lesser partisans were jailed or expelled as enemy aliens, West defended the colonial cause defiantly. While in the America he would never see again his boyhood neighbors froze and starved at Valley Forge, he promulgated his own Declaration of Independence and singlehandedly freed American art from the chains of British tradition. While William Penn's heirs sold their birthright for a pittance pension, he succeeded Sir Joshua Reynolds as president of the Royal Academy—retaining that august rank by acclamation during 27 of the most brilliant years in the annals of English painting.

In simple fact, West was the most successful American painter who ever lived—financially and in prestige with the great and popularity with the masses, overseas and at home. And while he climbed his own self-made ladder, he did more than any other expatriate to set artistic creation in motion in the America he left at 22.

Past 80 and still painting, he saw no marvel in his story; it fulfilled a prophecy. Thirteen days before his birth, he said, in the Friends' meeting house in Chester County, a visiting evangelist named Edmund Peckover preached so powerfully against the Old World's wickedness which the New World must cure, that his mother-to-be suffered premature labor pains and cried out, interrupting the sermon. "My father asked the preacher if this was not an omen. The preacher gripped his hand, and with emphatic solemnity said that a child sent into the world under such remarkable circumstances would prove no ordinary man."

The old are prone to gild the past, and in this instance, records show Reverend Peckover did not reach Pennsylvania until West was three years old. But so many agreed with West's own calm conviction of his extraordinariness that three Dukes, two Marquises, nine Earls, an Archbishop, four Bishops, and the Lord Mayor of London were in the throng of thousands that saw the Yankee Quaker laid to rest beside Sir Joshua Reynolds in St. Paul's Cathedral, March 11, 1820.

Benjamin West's Self Portrait *was painted in 1771.
(National Gallery)*

His father hoped he would be a preacher. But at six, left to mind a baby, he let it squawl while he limned its likeness with chalk his father used to tot up charges for ale and victuals. From then on, picture making was his life. Friendly Indians showed him how they mixed red and yellow earth to paint their faces. His mother gave him a lump of indigo with which she whitened her starched bonnets. He trapped his father's black tomcat, cut hair off its tail, and fitted the hairs into goose quills for a brush. Before long the cat was almost hairless.

Then a visitor from Philadelphia saw the products of West's untutored labors and sent him a box of oils, several prepared canvases, and six engravings. He copied the engravings, and sold the copies. At 13 he set up as a portraitist, going from farm to farm, finishing family groups in one sitting. At 16, he walked to Philadelphia, where he painted what he called "landskips" which he sold while the oil was wet and struck up acquaintance with Francis Hopkinson, the first American playwright.

Handsome and likeable, ill-educated but always learning by listening, he won influential friends. They said he should go to Europe to study. They might as well have advised him to fly to the moon. Still he scrimped and saved, until he fell in love with Elizabeth Shewell. Her people were well-off. They called him a vagabond and a pauper. Until he proved he could earn a living for two, he was not to see her again. Other youths in the throes of first romance might have weakened, but not Benjamin West. He got word to Elizabeth: "I am going away for a while. I will be back. Wait for me." Then he talked a grain ship owner into giving him deck passage to Italy.

He had a draft for 50 guineas which might not be collectible and some letters of introduction that might or might not be useful. As it turned out, he did not need them. "He was something new in Rome, and therefore interesting: a Quaker, a Yankee, probably a savage, certainly a curiosity. His self-assurance would have been offensive in a less attractive person. In him it was disarming. He knew absolutely nothing about literature or history, or even how to enter a drawing-room, but you forgave his ignorance when you watched him look at a painting." Thus wrote one stranger he met. Another, Thomas Robinson, an English aesthete who would one day be British Foreign Secretary, decided it would be amusing to present him to Cardinal Alessandro Albani, nephew of Pope Clement XI, who although blind was the arbiter of taste in the Imperial City.

The Cardinal saw with his fingertips. He ran them over West's features, then asked, "Is he white or black?" Told "He is very fair," His Eminence asked, "As fair as I am?" By next day, "as fair as the Cardinal" was a Roman catch phrase. But laughter died when the Cardinal sent for West to go with him on a tour of the Vatican Museum. A procession followed the disparate archetypes of the Old World and the New. Suddenly, West stopped, staring at the first nude statue he had ever seen, the *Apollo Belvedere*. "My God," he cried, "how like a Mohawk warrior!"

To hovering dilettantes, this was barbarian sacrilege. But the Cardinal had read Rousseau. "Come," he commanded, "and tell me about the Noble Red Man." Within the week, West was invited to study with Raphael Mengs, then *doyen* of Rome's painter-teachers. Mengs set him to copying and was amazed when he splashed paint without first drawing the composition. "Drawing outlines with the brush," said West, "is like playing the notes without a fiddle." When the Yankeeism was translated, Mengs muttered, then studied what West had put on canvas while he pondered, and let him go on with it. West's fame spread. "He does everything wrong but it works. He knows so little but he knows so much!"

He had his own opinion, expressed in his letters to Elizabeth in far-off Philadelphia. "The other students count leaves. I saw wood." Roman ladies coquetted. He was faithful. He sold pictures, at rising prices. Admirers of both sexes urged him not to think of returning to America. The year he had thought would be enough to learn what Europe could teach him stretched into two, then three. But in 1763, he started home, going by way of England so he could tell his father how much it had changed since John West joined the Quaker exodus to Pennsylvania. He can hardly have been surprised to find that a Yankee Quaker who called himself a painter was as much a *rara avis* in London as in Rome. But even Benjamin West cannot have expected Sir Joshua Reynolds to greet him as an equal.

Reynolds was England's premier portraitist, and London fashion's darling. A year before West's arrival he had brought about the forming of the Literary Club, of which Dr. Samuel Johnson, David Garrick, Oliver Goldsmith, James Boswell, Richard Brinsley Sheridan, Edmund Burke, and others almost as notable were members. After their first meeting, he sponsored West to this coterie, which could make or break careers with a few words or none. Reynolds was 40. West was 25. As long as they lived, they argued technique, but their friendship never waned. Hearing what paintings West had done in Rome, Reynolds said, "If you did those, remain in England. If not, get away to America as fast as you can." West put brush to canvas in swift strokes. Reynolds said, "Remain." West stayed.

Yet his climb began on ice, not at an easel. Back in Pennsylvania, he had been an expert skater. In London, on a Sunday afternoon, he went skating with Colonel William Howe, who would command the British Army during the Revolution still 13 years away. Before he knew it West was the center of an applauding crowd. Howe said, "A man who can skate like that must have talent," and led his cronies to West's studio. West's servant got 30 guineas in tips, but no one bought a picture. Still West sent for Elizabeth Shewell to come and marry him.

What ensued was argued angrily then and remains a matter of which witness you choose to believe. According to William White, first Episcopal Bishop of Pennsylvania, he and Francis Hopkinson learned that Elizabeth's people had locked her in her room, and went to Benjamin Franklin for advice. Franklin, the Bishop averred, joined in a conspiracy straight out of an old-style romance. Elizabeth's maid was bribed to hide a rope ladder under her dress and smuggled it to her mistress. Out a window and down the ladder went Elizabeth. Franklin, White, and Hopkinson waited with a curtained coach. After a wild drive through the night 16 miles down the river, they put her in a rowboat, which took her to a waiting schooner, and off she sailed to England and her Benjamin.

"Ben deserved a good wife," the Bishop said long afterward. "And old as I am, I am ready to do it again to serve such worthy people." According to him the Shewells never forgave Elizabeth, nor West, and refused all communication with them. But Matthew Pratt had a contradictory version. He said Elizabeth's relations raised no protest against her going and that he and West's father accompanied her to London.

Pratt, however, was West's first pupil, and painted himself and his mentor in *The American School* which hangs in the Metropolitan Museum. Back in Pennsylvania in 1768 after the first report that England had begun to call West "the Quaker Rembrandt," Pratt did well on the basis of his brief association with Pennsylvania's first famous native son; it would have been bad for business to admit that West had stolen a wife, especially since West made much of his Quaker probity and said he painted "to teach virtue."

This claim accelerated his climb in England. No less a guardian of morals than the Archbishop of York became his most devoted promoter, proposing a public subscription of 3,000 guineas "to enable Mr. West to devote all his time to painting history." Only half the fund was raised, but West had no need for subsidies. He was earning more than Joshua Reynolds or Thomas Gainsborough, merely from admission fees to view his *The Continence of Scipio, Pylades and Orestes, Cimon and Iphigenia, Diana and Endymion,* and—commissioned by the Archbishop—*Agrippina With the Ashes of Germanicus.*

The canvases were bed-sheet size, crowded, portentous, meticulously detailed, realistic yet unreal. They were pop art when George III reigned. There were no news pictures then. West supplied the lack. "West," James Flexner summarizes, "was an audience painter." He worked up heroics in his scenes to dramatize the glorious moment he knew his viewers wanted. Art's beauty to him was "perfect form selected from the bewildering midst of life's imperfections." Nature "was always raw and only antiquity sublime." West's spelling was also unique. His classical style, he wrote, "demands the greatest Cear and intelegance in History amaginable." It put yesterday's English idols in the shade. The Quaker Rembrandt admitted this with no false modesty. "When my pictures come into the exhibition, every other painter realizes that their sovereign is present."

Cannily, he kept up his skating performances. "Today I danced a minuet on skates . . . to the delight of the spectators." He was on the ice when word came from the Archbishop of York, summoning him posthaste to private audience with the King. They were to meet for minutes; instead, they talked for hours. "The King," Leigh Hunt sniffed subsequently, "would converse half a day at a time with the Yankee inkeeper's son, and beg, 'Come earlier and stay longer tomorrow.'" John Joshua Kirby, a proper Englishman, had been Painter to His Majesty. Now George III dismissed him and commissioned West to paint *The Departure of Regulus from Rome*.

From 1768 to 1804, in George III's eyes, the Yankee Quaker could do no wrong. Beginning with his *The Death of Wolfe* (now in Canada's National Gallery at Ottawa), he announced that contrary to enhallowed custom he would paint Wolfe and his officers in contemporary uniforms, not in Roman togas as tradition required. Joshua Reynolds warned him against affronting defenders of the status quo. West plunged ahead. *The Death of Wolfe*, when first exhibited, drew larger crowds than any other painting in British history. George III beamed. "West knows." He closed his doors to Lord Bute and Lord North, while he sat watching and questioning West, now at work on *William Penn's Treaty With the Indians*. This painting, on permanent exhibition in Philadelphia's Independence Hall, is probably West's masterpiece.

He was painting George III's portrait when a messenger brought news of the Declaration of Independence signed at Philadelphia. According to West the King said, "Well, if they can be happier under the government they have chosen than under mine, I shall be happy." No witness confirmed this. But there were witnesses, Loyalist refugees clamoring that the Yankee Quaker was too free with his tongue in praising the rebels, when the King silenced Lord Cathcart who called West a traitor, by declaiming from his throne, "A man who does not love his native land could never be a faithful subject of another, nor a true friend." His friendship for West was the deciding factor when Joshua Reynolds asked for permission to found the Royal Academy. West was one of its four founding members, and his vote made Reynolds its first president.

BENJAMIN WEST: THE QUAKER REMBRANDT

Eternally busy, in 13 years West completed and exhibited 33 wall-filling canvases. To help him picture *The Battle of La Hogue,* his royal friend ordered an admiral to take West to Spithead and turn out the British fleet. West sketched while frigates maneuvered in line of battle and their cannon fired blank charges. Next, the King commanded him to do 35 murals for Windsor Castle, "showing the progress of revealed religion." West set about this monumental task, but still found time to be one of few who praised the work of William Blake during that strange mystic's lifetime, and one of the first to give a hand-up to George Romney. "Every English painter of the generation, after Reynolds, owed something to Benjamin West."

"The instruction and encouragement the Quaker Rembrandt gave to young American painters during and after the Revolution made him the father of a dynasty." Charles Willson Peale from Maryland had been a saddler, coach builder, silversmith, taxidermist, dentist, and sculptor. West helped and taught him for two years. Back in America, Peale painted the first known portrait of Washington, served in the Continental Army, named his sons Raphaelle, Rembrandt, Rubens, and Titian, and made painters of all of them.

Ralph Earl from Massachusetts deserted his wife and children in 1779, studied with West in London, painted his way into the Royal Academy, acquired and deserted an English wife and family, and back in New England made "He has studied with Mr. West" his passport to prominence as a portraitist. Charles Bird King, one of the first Americans to specialize in painting Indians, was one of West's pupils. Another was William Dunlap, sometimes called "Father of American Drama." Joining West's American School in London in 1784, he returned to New York to write plays and operate theaters until bankruptcy drove him back to his easel. In 1826, he was a co-founder of the National

Benjamin West painted Colonel Guy Johnson *about 1775.*
(National Gallery)

Academy of Design. His tribute to West bears quoting. "He did rational historical illustrations, to be read like a book rather than experienced through direct emotion —as in his *Christ Healing the Sick*" (which has hung in the Pennsylvania Hospital in Philadelphia since 1817).

Washington Allston, one of whose aristocratic South Carolina relations married Theodosia, Aaron Burr's daughter, had written the class ode at Harvard, composed music, won acclaim as "a poet born with a book in his hand." After studying with West, he produced dramatic canvases including *The Feast of Belshazzar*, which was taken on tour in the Colonies and viewed by circus-sized crowds.

John Trumbull, son of an erstwhile Connecticut governor, "earned a reputation for being not only a genius but untruthful, mean, proud, and ambitious beyond forgiveness." He read Greek at six, graduated from Harvard as the youngest in his class, was aide-de-camp to Washington in 1778, and suddenly resigned "to go to London and learn from Mr. West." Benedict Arnold's treason and Major Andre's execution made London no place for Americans who had fought the British in uniform. Trumbull was jailed, and released only on West's intercession. Trumbull's West-styled magnum opus, *Capture of the Hessians at Trenton*, was so well liked by Americans that it was chosen to decorate the rotunda of the Capitol in Washington.

In 1775, Gilbert Stuart caught the last ship out of England, just before the British stormed Bunker Hill. In London he starved until West took him in. For four years, Stuart lived on West's courteously cloaked charity. With West's support and endorsement, he became London's most popular portraitist, working on six canvases simultaneously yet spending more than he earned, until to escape Debtors' Prison he decamped to Ireland.

By 1794 he was in Philadelphia, where he discovered George Washington. He had learned more than technique from West. Copying his master's methods of mass production, he turned out 75 repetitions of the so-called *Household Washington* (the original is in the Boston Museum of Fine Arts) and altogether some 111 variations of this and of the *Vaughn Washington* (in the National Gallery) and the *Lansdowne Washington* (in the Pennsylvania Academy of Fine Arts). He never ceased to thank the Yankee Quaker.

The list of those who had similar cause for gratitude that not all displayed could be much longer. It ends with Samuel F. B. Morse, who outlived him 52 years, still recalling how in 1810, when West at 72 was beginning all over again, "I was carried away by his competence and overcome by his kindness." To the very end, "any talented aspirant who lacked funds to finish becoming a painter could count on a loan from West, or even an invitation to become a guest in his house."

In 1805, at the zenith of his reign as Royal Academy president, "West voluntarily withdrew three of his canvases from the R. A. exhibition, to make room for some young unknowns whose pictures had been crowded out." In 1772, he had refused a knighthood. No Englishman would have risked offending George III by similar refusal. But far from taking umbrage he told West, "In spite of your Yankee independence, I will make you a peer when you finish your *History of Revealed Religion*." But then strange happenings began.

West painted a picture for the Queen, and at her request, "put in a lion to please little Prince Adolphus." Seeing this, suddenly the King began slashing the canvas. Soon after it was a Court secret. "His Majesty has gone stark mad." West was barred from seeing him. He had insisted on taking charge of West's money "to invest it where it would grow." But West had no written proof that the King owed him at least 20,000 guineas—a fortune in the times.

West's income sank to his pension of 1,000 guineas annually, while it cost him twice as much to maintain his studio and his American School. He wanted to go home to Pennsylvania, but could not for lack of funds and debts he would not leave unpaid. In 1800 he sent through the American Ambassador, Rufus King, his design for a monument to Washington. King took this to President Thomas Jefferson. It disappeared into some forgotten file. In 1801, West was notified that his commission to decorate Windsor Chapel, on which he had worked for 20 years, was canceled, and he would be paid nothing for his labors.

At long last he left London to go to France. Napoleon Bonaparte's lavish welcome and his election to the French Institute unleashed savage attack in England. West was excoriated for "his democratic spirit and lavish admiration of Bonaparte" and accused of having "plundered our King of 34,187 pounds sterling if not more." His wife was by now a helpless invalid. Lord Byron mocked "the dotard West, Europe's worst daub, poor England's best."

At 73, the Quaker Rembrandt struck back with the weapon that had never failed—his paintbrush. His *Christ Healing the Sick* sold for 15,000 guineas, after earning more than that from public exhibitions. He followed it with *Christ Rejected*, for which he refused 8,000 guineas. He got more. The insane King died, and England celebrated. West painted, and England cheered him on.

He was working on *Christ Looking at Peter After the Apostle's Denial* when at last and in a moment his strength failed. "Even in death his right hand kept the position of holding a brush." Churchmen refused to accept his body for burial because there was nothing to prove he had ever been baptized. Protest from high and low was so vehement that the English hierarchy decided an exception could be made in this one case.

BENJAMIN WEST: THE QUAKER REMBRANDT

No Americans were in the funeral cortege; those who had known the Quaker Rembrandt were too busy painting in the homeland he saw last 60 years before. In his studio, his old servant looked at empty benches where so many young Americans had learned their craft. "Ah, sir," he sighed, "where will they go now?" It is reasonable to guess that the innkeeper's son who conquered England with his brush would not have asked for a more eloquent obituary.

Aaron Burr (Culver)

THE AARON BURR AFFAIR

by Robert Hardy Andrews

This is a serious attempt to separate documented fact from myth and legend, to which reputable historians have contributed, regarding the tragic duel between Aaron Burr and Alexander Hamilton—a landmark in American political history. In the author's sincere opinion, a whole gallery of American heroes were guiltier than Burr—if what Burr did was a crime, as most Americans have been taught to believe.

Quite possibly, objective inquiry into a case long since marked closed to the satisfaction of most judges after-the-fact invites indignant rebuttal from those who think that what they prefer to think is therefore gospel.

However this risk seems worthwhile, if even a few are willing to hear a summing-up for the defense 163 years after a duel that need never had been fought destroyed the victor while it only killed the loser.

THE AARON BURR AFFAIR

On the bright morning of July 11, 1804, a farm boy from Connecticut walked wide-eyed along the busy streets of little old New York, nerving himself for a courtesy call on his famous cousin. The house in Greenwich loomed before him like a castle. Facing a Negro in black satin livery, he asked "Is Colonel Burr at home?" as if he half-hoped the answer would be "no."

Alexis, body servant to the Vice President of the United States, was used to visitors hesitant on his master's doorstep. Smiling, he shepherded the awed youth through severely elegant rooms, hung with paintings mostly by the American Da Vinci, John Vanderlyn. In a library that overflowed with books, a small, neat, strikingly handsome man sat reading a volume of Voltaire.

What followed was told by Burr's cousin from that day until he died. "Neither in Colonel Burr's manner nor in his conversation was there any evidence of excitement or concern. Except the master of the house, not a soul in Richmond Hill knew aught yet of that morning's work; nor indeed could it be said in any sense of the word that the master himself knew what he had done." The man who expected to be President after Thomas Jefferson's second term in the White House shook hands and led his unexpected guest into the dining room.

"The conversation was quite in the ordinary strain, Burr inquiring after friends and the youth giving the information sought. After a leisurely repast, Burr bade him good-morning. The youth strolled off toward the city, which he reached about 10 o'clock. As he strolled down the Broad-way, he fancied he observed in passers-by the sign that something extraordinary had happened or was expected. Near Wall-street, an acquaintance rushed up to him, breathless, and said 'Colonel Burr has killed General Hamilton in a duel this morning'."

Ever since that morning, what actually occurred "at

THE AARON BURR AFFAIR

a place called Weahawk across the Hudson in Jersey," just how it happened, and above all, why, has been disputed. There is full agreement only on one fact that cannot be questioned: The first Secretary of the Treasury of the United States and the first Vice President elected by Tammany and by what would become the Democratic Party faced each other with pistols at ten paces. Alexander Hamilton fell mortally wounded, while Aaron Burr left the Field of Honour unscathed. Even this is not necessarily the whole truth.

It might have been much better for Burr, if he, not Hamilton, had been the loser of the life-or-death encounter that was inevitable from their first meeting. Years later, when even Burr admitted he had lived a generation too long, he said, "If I had read Sterne more, and Voltaire less, I would have realized there was room on earth for both General Hamilton and Colonel Burr." However, he is not known to have quoted what was said a moment after the fatal shot was fired. "Colonel Burr," said his chief second, William Van Ness, with startling prescience, "you have just made General Hamilton a great man."

So he had done, no matter what he had intended. The cult of Hamilton the martyr has gained more intolerant disciples constantly, while it has become an article of the American credo that Burr was first a murderer, and then a traitor. That neither judgment does justice to the record must be blamed on American historians who, almost without exception, in the case of *Hamilton vs. Burr*, lay themselves open to inquiry pursuant to Benjamin Franklin's dictum that "Historians relate not what was done but what they prefer to think was done."

Napoleon thought "History is a fable agreed upon." Lord Chesterfield warned his sons, "History is a heap of confused facts." The dying Robert Walpole asked his friends to read him "Anything about history, for history must be false." These three wry cynics were required reading, in the remarkable course of study Burr laid out for his famously beautiful and accomplished daughter, whom he christened Theodosia—"which I take to mean the Gift of God."

For himself, he taught her by precept and demonstration that "History, like the law, is whatever is plausibly proclaimed and persistently maintained," to which he added from subsequent experience, "Increasingly, as the body of precedent is enlarged, history, like the law, becomes a science of obfuscation."

All things considered, he must have foreseen that history—or at least those who put it on paper—would proclaim and maintain the worst about him, not the best. But his lifelong maxim was "Never apologize, never explain." It is doubtful that he would give thanks for an effort to re-examine the body of evidence, 163 years *post facto*. Still with another national election about to test the two-party system that owes more to Aaron Burr than Alexander Hamilton, a fact which neither Democratic nor Republican candidates are likely to recall in campaign speeches, it seems a proper time to point out what went unmentioned in his times—that Burr was never given the benefit of reasonable doubt.

Burr used this recourse often, as the highest-paid and most redoubtable courtroom pleader in his era. It was his secret weapon, suddenly revealed, when Alexander Hamilton was his co-counsel for the defense in New York's first sensational murder trial. That was early on in 1800, but not long before Burr and Thomas Jefferson tied in the vote for President to succeed John Adams who loathed them both. Only Burr's refusal to purchase support offered to him on a silver serving-tray broke the tie and gave the White House key to Jefferson.

Hamilton's letters make it clear he did everything he could to destroy John Adams and concurrently blacken

Alexander Hamilton

Burr and undermine Jefferson. He was on this course when for reasons still mysterious he consented to join Burr in defending a certain Levi Weeks, accused of drowning Juliana Elmore Sands, known as the Angel of Greenwich Village, in a well which by strange coincidence Burr owned on Spring Street in Manhattan, the night before Christmas Eve, 1799.

For once they stood together, on the unpopular side, for New York wanted Levi Weeks sent to the gallows. In fact, as spectators soon realized, they dueled in court; the defendant was hardly more than an onlooker. To a point, they were much alike. Both were small, with a genius for walking tall. Both were fastidious, punctilious, and impetuous. Both attracted women, and were attracted to them. Both believed implicitly in their right, and their responsibility, to lead.

Hamilton was the younger, by a year—if, that is, his own count was correct. If he erred by a few months, his enemies whispered, then he was not, as he insisted, the illegitimate son of the ne'er-do-well son of a Scottish Lord, but legitimately the son of John Lavien or Levine, a Danish merchant in the West Indies.

No such cloud was cast on Burr's ancestry. His grandfather, the Calvinist theologian Jonathan Edwards, was president of the College of New Jersey which would become Princeton University. His father, the Reverend Aaron Burr, succeeded Jonathan Edwards as president at Princeton and Burr was born there, in Nassau Hall in 1756. He graduated there and is buried there, although this is not always noted in Princeton guidebooks. Good things came to him easily.

Not so for Hamilton. Arriving in New York at 15, he was able to attend King's College (now Columbia University) only through the aid of friends who pitied him. But at 20 he was a Lieutenant-Colonel on General George Washington's staff; at 30, he was co-author of the Federalist Papers; by 1789, he was the first Secretary of the Treasury; and at 43, he headed the Federalist Party, was Inspector General of the Armies, and had succeeded in electing his father-in-law, wealthy General Philip Schuyler, to the seat Burr had held as Senator from New York.

Burr, too, had been a Lieutenant-Colonel. He was at Valley Forge in 1777, Senator in 1791. But Hamilton had been heard to say "Burr is a finished failure." Still, on a wintry day in January, 1800, the fated opposites united in a fight to save the life of a creature both despised. It was Hamilton who raised the issue of reasonable doubt, citing precedents while the jurors dozed.

Then it was Burr's turn to sum up. He did so with the sudden flashing flamboyance that had caused Hamilton to describe him as a charlatan, "a very Caesar." Snatching a candelabra from the judge's bench, he blew out all the candles. Then he seized the only other candelabra that lighted the courtroom, blew out all candles but one, and dashed from one to the other of the startled spectators, jurors, and eyewitnesses. "Tell me," he challenged the jury, "as God is your judge, could you swear on your life that in a snowstorm, at ten paces, you could positively identify a murderer?"

Without leaving the courtroom, the jurors voted "Not guilty." Burr, not Hamilton, had won. But the dead girl's aunt, pushing forward through the chattering crowd, chose Hamilton, not Burr, as the object of curse. "If there is a God in Heaven, thee will not die a natural death!" And the chain of events had begun, that led inexorably to a place called Weehawken.

Textbooks and reference works almost unanimously infer, if they do not declare in so many words, that in 1800, when Hamilton came into the open as his unrelenting foe, Burr was already on the road to premeditated homicide. There is, however, not a scintilla of evidence that any court would accept that murder was ever in Burr's mind.

He stood trial only once—at Richmond, Virginia, in

1807, charged with treason. Chief Justice John Marshall, presiding, had liked Hamilton and loathed Burr. Most of the jurors were in similar case. President Jefferson demanded Burr's conviction, insisting the nation was in clear and present danger because of him.

The principal prosecution witness, General James Wilkinson, commanded the American Army in the West. That he was also, then and for long afterward, a paid spy for Spain, who had promised his employers to keep the United States from taking Texas, is another story. In simple justice, as honorable men, Chief Justice Marshall and the jurors found Burr "Not guilty." That they also played Pilate, washing their hands while they surrendered Burr to the mob, is also another story. We are concerned here with Burr's self-destruction, for that is what resulted from his duel with Hamilton.

Was it murder? At worst, his plea of *non liquet*, not proven, would be sustained by any court of appeals. But he never entered any plea. He was indicted, but quite illegally, by a rump jury sitting in New York reviewing events alleged to have transpired out of its jurisdiction in New Jersey; the sole witness admitted his testimony was all hearsay. Convicting Burr was so far out of the question that his deadliest foes were careful not to hale him into court. No belated discovery of new evidence, suppressed or overlooked, needs to be claimed now.

A solid case for the defense can rest entirely on information always accessible, albeit buried under a mound of myth and prejudice. If it is heard, Americans as congenital practitioners of fair play can hardly fail to look askance at self-elected judges who improved on Burr's own courtroom technique of obfuscation to hide the glaring flaw in their verdict—which is that they always try Burr, but never Hamilton.

As much today as when Burr was the country's cleverest criminal lawyer, both precedent and common law protect all men equally against being punished for crimes not in the statute books. In the time of Burr and Hamilton, none of the United States had yet outlawed the *Code Duello*. On the contrary, hallowed tradition made it inescapably obligatory for gentlemen to give satisfaction in single combat to other gentlemen who demanded it. Preachers in their pulpits excepted dueling from the Fifth Commandment—if only because so many deacons were duelists.

Looking back from the eminence of our present respect for the sanctity of human life, we may say that if neither Burr nor Hamilton did anything better for their country, together they shocked our great-great-grandfathers into doing away with an inexcusable institution. But calling your man out and killing him or being killed was *noblesse oblige*, not murder, when Burr and Hamilton met for the last time at Weehawken.

William Pitt as England's prime minister felt he must either fight or resign and chose the lesser evil. He traded shots at sunrise with his Master of the Mint. Even Benjamin Franklin, as American plenipotentiary in England before the Revolution, was threatened with a challenge, and though he found means to avoid the issue he did not castigate the custom.

John Paul Jones ("I have just begun to fight!"), Stephen Decatur ("My country right or wrong!"), Charles Cotesworth Pinckney ("Millions for defense but not one damned penny for tribute!"), Henry Clay ("I had rather be right than President!")—the roster of American duelists is lengthy and illustrious, before and after Burr and Hamilton. And certainly any chronicler of the Burr-Hamilton tragedy invites suspicion if, as many have, he pictures Burr as a pistol-waving firebrand, but Hamilton as hesitant, from moral principles, to appear on the so-called Field of Honour.

In December, 1778, Hamilton stigmatized General Charles Lee's conduct at the Battle of Monmouth as "monstrous and unpardonable." He did this in full knowledge that Lee had come to the colonies only because he had to flee Europe after killing an Italian officer in a duel. Testifying at Lee's court-martial, Hamilton charged "rank cowardice."

When Lee failed to take up this gage of battle, Hamilton announced "If I cannot force him to challenge me, I will challenge him." He was forestalled by his friend, Colonel John Laurens. It was then agreed between them that Hamilton would serve as Lauren's second, with the proviso that if Laurens fell Hamilton would demand satisfaction from Lee "and avenge both Laurens and General Washington."

Lee and Laurens fought near the Four-Mile Stone on Point-No-Point road as arranged by their seconds, Hamilton and a Major Edwards. They fired simultaneously, at six paces. Lee claimed a wound, but demanded a second exchange. Hamilton recorded that "I observed the matter really should not go farther, but I was too tender of my friend's honour to persist in opposing it." However Lee's second prevailed, and "The affair terminated as it was then circumstanced."

Hamilton immediately after published a *Narration* in which he commented, "We think it a piece of justice to the two gentlemen to declare that, after they met, their conduct was strongly marked with all the politeness, generosity, coolness, and firmness, that ought to characterize a transaction of this kind."

Nor did passing years diminish Hamilton's uncritical respect for the *Code Duello* as made and provided. When Commodore Nicholson of New York alleged that Hamilton, while Secretary of the Treasury, secretly invested a hundred thousand pounds in British securities just before John Jay negotiated a treaty favorable to Great Britain which Hamilton had drafted, Hamilton threatened publicly to demand from Nicholson "that satisfaction to which an insulted gentleman is entitled."

Again, he was forestalled. De Witt Clinton, a member of Hamilton's Federalist inner circle, challenged Nicholson. A never explained "accommodation" averted their duel. Helped into the Senate by Hamilton, Clinton fought two victorious duels while he was a Senator.

One of these was a vicious shooting-match with John Swartwout, a New York Assemblyman, one of the activists belonging to what Hamilton called *Burr's Myrmidons*. Hit in the right leg, Swartwout stood firm and, while a surgeon dug Clinton's bullet out of his leg, demanded another exchange. Clinton obliged, and put a bullet through Swartwout's other leg.

Trumpeting "I wish I had the principal here, and not his underling," Clinton departed, to be heroized next day in pro-Hamilton newspapers. There is no showing of any criticism by Hamilton. It would have come very strangely from him in view of events in Philadelphia, then the national capital, in the winter of 1796.

Philadelphia buzzed with scandal. Hamilton was accused of adultery with a Mrs. Marie Reynolds and was alleged to have paid blackmail to her complaisant husband. He published another *Narration* in which he did not deny the charges, but rang changes on Adam's "The woman tempted me, and I sinned." Indignantly, he denounced Senator James Monroe—who was about to become Minister to France and had his sights set on the White House—of conduct unbecoming a gentleman, in that he had something to do with permitting the Reynolds affidavits to reach the press and public. Accompanied by John Barker Church, his brother-in-law, Hamilton called on Monroe, called him a scoundrel, and—Monroe said—shouted "Go home and get your pistols; I am ready to meet you!"

Hamilton and Church, contrarily, averred that it was Monroe who wanted to duel. That one impended is clear. Monroe asked Burr to come from Albany and serve as his second. Belying the reputation since fas-

The duel between Burr and Hamilton. (Culver)

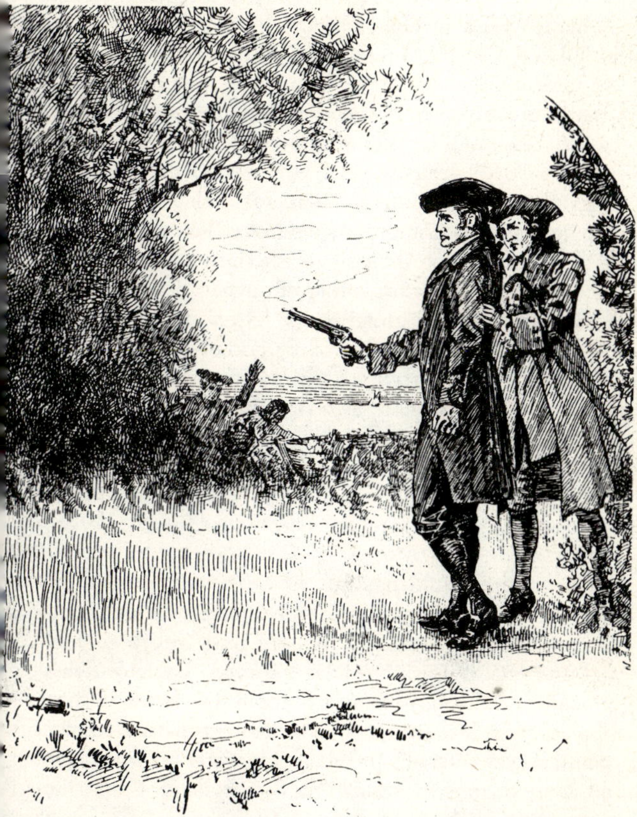

tened on him, Burr said there must be no duel.

Burr was a widower. Hamilton was an uxorious family man, with a lovely, rich, and loyal wife. Yet he had circulated many confidential letters accusing Burr of multiple adulteries. Now with no apparent awareness that pots should not call kettles black, Hamilton continued to accuse Burr—though never to his face—of illicit amours with various women, this while Burr was working out an accommodation that left both Hamilton and Monroe with honor untarnished. As Burr explained it: "I found it not too difficult to convince them both that we cannot afford to lose either of them."

If Hamilton was grateful, his letters do not show it. His star was falling while Burr's rose. Suddenly Burr was Vice President, with a good chance of being President next time around, and Hamilton's Federalist monolith disintegrated. The end began when a Federalist faction, preferring Burr to Jefferson, deserted Hamilton and offered the presidency to Burr. "He had only to suborn a couple of personages who were eager to be suborned."

That Burr would not buy or be bought ground salt into Hamilton's wounds. In the opinion of many, he was as finished then as he thought Burr was three years before. And if Burr is to be believed, he took defeat gracefully. When Burr asked about his letter writing, "he blamed his attacks on excitement natural during political campaigns," and gave his word he would pen no more communications "in the style of Cicero denouncing Catiline."

No witnesses recorded any such discussion and agreement. But Burr's intelligence system was much too well organized for him to have gone in ignorance until 1844 of continuing written accusations, any one of which could have been seized upon as sufficient grounds for a challenge under the *Code Duello*. That he took no umbrage publicly was explained subsequently by his *Myrmidons* as the victor's patience with the vanquished.

Or it may have been, of course, that Burr practiced the adaptation he had found so useful in courtrooms, where he turned unfriendly witnesses to account by paraphrasing Hamlet's *"The lady doth protest too much, methinks."* Or, again, quite possibly he was too engrossed in climbing higher to lose time on a bypath. Definitely the *Code Duello* was no part of his weaponry, at least not at this stage. Contrasted to Hamilton's known dossier, only one challenge and one encounter were credited to Burr before the interview on the heights at Weehawken.

In 1799, by sub rosa politicking, Burr managed passage at Albany of a New York Waterworks Bill, creating a Manhattan Company through which he proposed to provide Manhattan with a complex of pipelines that would end enforced reliance on inadequate and contaminated wells. On the surface, this was a noble cause. But fine print in the bill legalized the Bank of the Manhattan Company—which would smash the money monopoly held until then by the Bank of the United States, which Hamilton had founded.

Hamilton's brother-in-law, John Barker Church—to whose adventures and misadventures in England during the Revolution and in the United States after independence a specialist in high and low finance could easily devote more than one fat volume—went around Manhattan's taverns charging Burr with "bribery and corruption." Burr called the charges "absolute and damnable lies" and challenged—which is what Church said he had hoped and worked for all along.

If Hamilton made any attempt to prevent this duel, no one remembered it. He left that city the night before Church faced Burr and did not return until the following Sunday. Before the word to "Fire!" was given, Burr is said to have discovered his pistol had been misloaded and was useless. Church put a bullet through his coattails. Then Burr reloaded unhurriedly, murmuring, "My shot now."

Church decamped, leaving Burr's marksmanship untested. Brother lawyers who had ridden the up-state circuit with Burr said this was just as well. In target shooting to pass the time, they said they learned that "Burr could not hit a barn-door in less than three tries."

But if crooked, clownish Church made a farce of punctilio that Hamilton had always taken seriously, stark tragedy soon took the stage. Fighting with his back to the wall in November, 1801, Hamilton founded the New York *Evening Post* as a political rostrum and chose as its first editor a brother attorney, William Coleman who, like Hamilton, had once though briefly been Burr's law partner.

Previously Hamilton had been served in his unremitting crusade against Burr by, among others, a personage called James Cheetham, exiled from England for publishing libels, whose *American Citizens* sold its scandals to the highest bidder. Cheetham now turned from blackening Burr to threatening Coleman.

Contemptuously, Coleman declined "to give a gentleman's satisfaction to a creature of Cheetham's known character." Captain William Thompson, the swashbuckling New York harbor master, took up Cheetham's quarrel. Both parties bandied Hamilton's name, but he did not intervene. Coleman and Thompson fired at each other in a blinding snowstorm. Thompson fell. Dying, before he was carried away, he swore all present to secrecy—thus adhering to the *Code Duello* by protecting the victor and the seconds from improbable prosecution or quite possible reprisal.

Details of the encounter cannot have been unknown to Hamilton, who again that evening dictated editorial to Coleman at The Grange, the mansion he had designed so that its veranda had a fine view of the Palisades—and Weehawken—across the Hudson. And it is reasonable to suppose that Coleman may have been a hero to emulate, in the estimation of Philip, Hamilton's beloved son, just graduated from Columbia College at 18.

"His father," one of Hamilton's colleagues said regarding Philip, "is certain of his future greatness but alas Philip is a sad rake and I have serious doubts whether he would ever be an honour to his family or his country." As Burr had done with his only daughter, training her to be an extension of himself, so Hamilton sought to do with Philip. His Spartan schedule for his son called for rising not later than six in the morning between April 1 and October 1, not later than seven the other months of the year. Philip must read law each day until nine, then be in his father's office until dinner time, then read law again until five, and resume after supper at seven, and be in bed by ten. On Saturdays, he was allowed liberty from noon until sundown. But Philip had begun to drink, and loved the theater, and yearned to prove himself "as more than 'General Hamilton's son.'"

On a November night in 1801, Philip and a youth named Price looked for excitement and found it. At the New York Theater they exchanged audible insulting remarks about George Eacker, a Burr supporter. Eacker snapped something about "a damned rascal." Whomever he meant, both Philip and Price immediately challenged him.

Price fought Eacker first, on a Sunday, at Powles Hook. The encounter was bloodless and therefore unsatisfactory. Now it was Philip's turn—unless his father should step in. But though days passed, during which the matter was noised about the town, it appears that Hamilton took no steps to save his son.

Philip and Eacker met on November 23. At the first fire, Eacker's bullet wounded Philip fatally. Philip's sister, Angelica, went mad with grief and remained hopelessly insane until she died half a century afterward. Philip's mother never recovered from stunned heartbreak. Hamilton was beside himself, but no arrest was made, or even suggested, however Hamilton felt now about the *Code Duello*.

Nor does it appear that any of Hamilton's associates thought it proper to ask for an inquest. Burr said he went to Hamilton, to express his sympathy. There is no question that during this period Burr and Hamilton met frequently, dined at each other's houses, borrowed small sums from each other, and seemingly had arrived at truce if not at fondness.

Still all the while Hamilton was writing and circulating letters, declaring "Burr is bankrupt financially and morally"—though from past experience he could scarcely have imagined Burr would fail to lay hands on copies of his diatribes. "Mine is an odd destiny," he wrote to Gouverneur Morris. "Perhaps no man in the United States has sacrificed or done more for the present Constitution than myself; and contrary to all my anticipations of its fate, as you know from the very beginning, I am still labouring to prop the frail and worthless fabric. Yet I have the murmurs of its friends no less than the curses of its foes for my reward. What can I do better than withdraw from the scene? Every day proves to me more and more, that the American world was not made for me."

James Parton, who interviewed many old men who were then young and keen, watching and listening close by while Burr and Hamilton played the last act of their drama, wrote that "It was in 1802 that Colonel Burr, having obtained some imperfect knowledge of Hamilton's usual mode of characterizing him, had a conversation with him on that subject. Hamilton (so said Burr in later years) had explained, apologized, and left upon his mind the impression, never effaced, that henceforth Hamilton was pledged to refrain from speaking of him as he had been accustomed to do. They parted with cordiality, and had ever since been, apparently, very good friends. Burr considered then, and always, that he had made prodigious sacrifices, as a man of honour and a gentleman, for the sake of avoiding a hostile meeting that could not but injure both as candidates for the public confidence."

Parton, a hundred years closer to the actual events than we are now, is sometimes dismissed as too much a special pleader for Burr, even by those who draw most heavily on Parton's research. However, his summing-up seems more judicious than prejudicial. "Consider," he argued, "the force of another circumstance upon a mind like Burr's whose religion was fidelity to comrades. Men who proudly looked up to him as more than their political chief—as the pre-eminent gentleman, and model man-of-the-world, of that age—had fought in his quarrel, and fought with a reckless courage which he at first inspired, and then commanded. If the occasion should arise, could chief decline the encounter with chief, after the subalterns had so gallantly contended? And this consideration had equal weight with Hamilton. Beside having sanctioned the practice of dueling, by serving as second to Colonel Laurens in his duel with General Lee, his own son had fallen, in what the language of that day called the vindication of his father's honor. In short, never since the *Code Duello* was invented, were two men, if the requisite technical provocation should arise, so peculiarly and irresistibly bound to fight, as were Aaron Burr and Alexander Hamilton in the summer of 1804."

Surely there was a feel of inevitability in the slow march toward Weehawken that followed Burr's decision on June 18, 1804, when he sent a formal note to Hamilton by hand of William Van Ness—one day to be Chief Justice of New York. "Sir," Burr wrote, "I send for your perusal a letter signed Charles D. Cooper, which, although apparently published some time ago, has but very recently come to my knowledge. Mr. Van Ness, who does me the favour to deliver this, will point out to you that clause of the letter to which I particularly request your attention. You must perceive, sir, the necessity of a prompt and unqualified acknowledgement of denial of the use of any expression that would warrant the assertions of Dr. Cooper."

Hamilton replied on June 20. "Sir: I have maturely reflected on the subject of your letter, and the more I have reflected, the more I have become convinced, that I could not, without manifest impropriety, make the avowal or disavowal which you seem to think necessary. The clause pointed out by Mr. Van Ness is in these terms: 'I could detail to you *a still more despicable opinion* which General Hamilton *has expressed* of Mr. Burr.'

"To endeavour to discover the meaning of this declaration, I was obliged to seek in the antecedent part of this letter for the opinion to which it referred, as having been already disclosed. I found it in these words: 'General Hamilton and Judge Kent have declared *in substance*, that they looked upon Mr. Burr to be a *dangerous man*, and *one who ought not to be trusted with the reins of government.*'" The italics are Hamilton's.

He had said worse of Burr uncounted times, since their predestined rivalry began in 1777. Then why did Burr wait until 1804 to call a halt at last? Readers are usually given to understand he had simply and suddenly decided to eliminate the one unconquerable adversary who still barred his path to capture of the country. But if truth, like the world, is round, not flat, then a look at it from another view raises reasonable doubt.

Hamilton's confession to Gouverneur Morris was not mere breast beating. His shifts and stratagems, aimed to get rid of Jefferson and Burr, had instead left his party shattered and nearly obliterated. Never comfortable before a jury, Hamilton's credit as a master of compromise and out-of-court settlement had suffered through a series of failures.

His home life was a horror for one of his sensitivity: his mad daughter screaming, his wife a wraith, his sister-in-law professedly in love with him, his brother-in-law enmeshed in lawsuits and head over heels in debt, his own financial affairs so tangled that he borrowed even from Burr. No one—Burr least of all—had anything to gain from harming him further. It would be crueler to let him alone.

But now he played *Yea-and-Nay* with strange recklessness. "It is evident," he wrote to Burr, "that the phrase, 'still more despicable', admits of infinite shades. How am I to judge of the degree intended? Or how shall I annex any precise idea to language so indefinite? Between gentlemen, *despicable* and *still more despicable* are not worth the pains of distinction; when, therefore, you do not interrogate me as to the opinion which is specifically ascribed to me, I must conclude, that you view it as within the limits to which the animadversions of political components upon each other may justifiably extend, and consequently as not warranting the idea of it which Dr. Cooper appears to entertain." Again, the italics are Hamilton's.

His comment continued for several very long paragraphs, recalling the remark of a jurist who studied Hamilton and Burr as co-counsel in the Tea-Water Well murder trial. "It takes Hamilton an hour to reach the point that Burr takes care of in a sentence." Hamilton was never more prolix than in this late debate with Burr.

"I stand," he wrote, "ready to avow or disavow, promptly and explicitly, any precise or definite opinion which I may be charged with having declared to any gentleman. More than this cannot fitly be expected of me; and especially it cannot be expected that I shall enter into an explanation upon a basis so vague as that which you have adopted. I trust on more reflection you will see the matter in the same light with me. If not, I *can only regret the circumstances and must abide the consequences.*" In this instance, the italics are the author's.

Under the *Code Duello*, Hamilton had in thirteen words negated the thousand that preceded them. He had used almost the identical sentence too often before, not to be aware that their import to Burr must be *the next move is yours*. If Burr was as bloody minded as the prosecution paints him, procedure from this moment was automatic—and the *Code Duello*, not even under his control.

Van Ness, as his second, would deliver a cartel. Hamilton's second would receive it. Time, place, weapons, number of paces between the duelists would be settled without their presence. Then the principals would be notified. But Burr—not Hamilton—temporized. His letter of June 21 essayed to open the door Hamilton had closed.

"Sir," he wrote, "your letter of the 20th instant has this day been received. Having considered it attentively, I regret to find in it nothing of that sincerity and delicacy which you profess to value. Political opposition can never absolve gentlemen from the necessity of a rigid adherence to the laws of honour and the rules of decorum. I neither claim such privilege nor indulge it in others.

"The time 'when' is in your own knowledge, but in no way material to me, as the calumny has now first been disclosed, so as to become the subject of my notice, and as the effect is present and palpable. Your letter has furnished me with new reasons for requiring a definite reply." Which can be read as saying no, *the next move is not mine; it is still yours*. And Hamilton appears to have agreed.

"Sir," Hamilton wrote to Burr on June 22, "your first letter, in a style too peremptory, made a demand, in my opinion, unprecedented and unwarrantable. My answer, pointing out the embarrassment, gave you an opportunity to take a less exceptionable course. You have not chosen to do it; but by your last letter received this day, containing expression *indecorous* and *improper*, you have increased the difficulties to explanation intrinsically incident to the nature of your application. If by a 'definite reply,' you mean the direct avowal or disavowal required in your first letter, I have no other answer to give, than that which has already been given." Here again, the italics are Hamilton's.

And while Burr was reading what was at the very least defiance, Hamilton called in Nathaniel Pendleton and told him "I have told Mr. Van Ness that I consider Mr. Burr's second communication rude and offensive, and unless it is recalled, the only answer it is possible for me to make is that Mr. Burr must take such steps as he may think proper." In essence, he refused to avoid invocation of the *Code Duello*.

Whatever the prosecution deduces, Pendleton—who was there—thought Hamilton was determined on a duel and reasoned with him worriedly until Hamilton permitted the drawing-up of a paper "containing what General Hamilton is willing to concede." This stated in generalities that to the best of his recollection, whatever he might have said against Burr "consisted of comments on the political principles and views of Colonel Burr, and the results that might be expected from them in the event of his election as Governor, without reference to any particular instance of past conduct, or to private character." It was hardly a soft answer turning wrath away. Nor was the second paper.

"The conversation to which Dr. Cooper alluded," it said, "turned wholly on political topics, and did not attribute to Colonel Burr any instance of dishonourable conduct, or relate to his private character, and in relation to any other language or conversation of General Hamilton which Mr. Burr will specify, a prompt and frank avowal or disavowal will be made." He would not retreat an inch from his position, that no politician should be called to account for anything he might say against a rival politician.

But the difference he defended, between politician and gentleman, was what Burr declined to see. He had been quoted, long before, as having "said with a wry smile, that General Hamilton's weakness was that he tried so very hard to be a gentleman." It was not a remark that legitimized a challenge, but Hamilton had never forgiven it.

Now Burr replied: "When and where injurious opinions and expressions have been uttered by General Hamilton must be best known to him, and of him only will Colonel Burr inquire. No denial or declaration will be satisfactory, unless it be general, so as to wholly exclude the idea that rumours derogatory to Colonel Burr's honour have originated with General Hamilton, or have been fairly inferred from anything he has said.

"A definite reply to a requisition of this nature was demanded by Colonel Burr's on the 21st inst. This being refused, invites the alternative alluded to in General Hamilton's letter of the 20th." Let it be noted for the re-opened record, that the actual author of his communication was not Burr, but William Van Ness—acting in his capacity under the *Code Duello* which, as he maintained ever after, not Burr but Hamilton invoked.

And Pendleton spoke similarly for Hamilton, in replying on June 27 that "If the alternative alluded to is definitively tendered, it must be accepted; the time, place, and manner to be afterward regulated." To this Pendleton appended Hamilton's request for only enough time in which to complete his cases then pending in the Circuit Court, and "respecting my own affairs."

Although no formal challenge had been certified by the seconds, all New York then knew that Burr and Hamilton would fight. No voice was lifted in protest. On the contrary, while days dragged, all concerned kept their own counsel. On July 4, Hamilton completed and sealed a *Letter To My Wife* to be placed in her hands and opened only in the event of his death. In this, he stated he had endeavoured "by all honourable means" to avoid the duel, and that he would not survive it. But those who watched him that evening, at the Independence Day dinner of the Society of the Cincinnati of which both he and Burr were charter members, wrote after July 11 that Hamilton's actions were scarcely those of a man who walked in the shadow of imminent death.

Colonel Trumbull, for one, wrote in his diary of meeting both Burr and Hamilton at the celebration. "The singularity of their manner was observed by all, though few had any suspicion of the cause; Burr was silent, gloomy, sour; Hamilton entered with glee into all the gayety of a convivial party, and even sang a military song."

Both men then went home to write their wills. Hamilton's testament is seldom quoted in full. Burr's gets even shorter shrift, if any. Yet objective appraisal of contrast between the two documents may reveal more about the signatories and their intentions than anything either had set down for posterity before this time.

Hamilton instructed his executors to sell his assets and if possible, pay his debts, and to give the residue, "if any there shall be," to his wife, Elizabeth Schuyler Hamilton. He continued with *Remarks,* so headed, "explanatory of his conduct, motives, and views" in agreeing to meet Burr with pistols. "I am conscious," he declared, "of no *ill-will* to Colonel Burr"—the italics are his—"distinct from political opposition, which, as I trust, has proceeded from pure and upright motives."

Continuing, he said "I shall hazard much, and can possibly gain nothing, by the issue of the interview. But it was, as I conceive, impossible for me to avoid it." He would not deny "that my animadversions on the political principles, character, and views of Colonel Burr have been extremely severe; and on different occasions, I, in common with many others, have made very unfavourable criticisms on particular instances of the private conduct of this gentleman. In proportion as these impressions were entertained with sincerity, and uttered with motives and for purposes which might appear to me to be commendable, would be the difficulty (until they could be removed by evidence of their being erroneous) of explanation or apology."

To Burr, in days ahead, what Hamilton wrote in a letter that might never be opened "read like the confessions of a penitent monk." It was harsh judgment, but this might be excused in view of what ensued. "I am not sure," Hamilton wrote, "whether, under all the circumstances, I did not go further in the attempt to accommodate, than a punctilious delicacy will justify. If so, I hope the motives I have stated will excuse me. It is not my design, by what I have said, to affix any odium on the conduct of Colonel Burr, in this case."

Never apologize, never explain. Burr's testament made no mention whatever of the impending duel, of Hamilton, or of his hope and motives. He instructed Theodosia to burn all his private papers that, "if by accident made public, would injure any person." His estate, he said, would barely pay his debts, "I mean if I should die this year." Meticulously, he listed personal bequests: a Vanderlyn painting to the orphaned girl who had grown up with Theodosia, fifty dollars in cash to a Negro servant "as a reward for her fidelity," his wearing apparel and a sword or a pair of pistols to his body servant.

"Dispose of Nancy as you please. She is honest, robust, and good-tempered. Peter is the most intelligent and best-disposed black I have ever known. (I mean the black boy I bought last Fall from Mr. Trumbull.) I advise you, by all means, to keep him as the valet of your son." In an afterthought he added, "It just now occurs to me to give Frederic my watch," and "The seal of the late General Washington, you may keep for your son, or give it to whom you please."

Legacies catalogued, he concluded: "I am indebted to you, my dearest Theodosia, for a very great portion of the happiness which I have enjoyed in this life. You have completely satisfied all that my heart and affections had hoped or even wished. With a little more perseverance and industry, and determination, you will obtain all that my ambition or vanity had fondly imagined. Let your son have occasion to be proud that he had a mother. Adieu. Adieu. A. Burr."

That he ended thus, with no reference to what had occurred, or might occur next morning, has been interpreted as a cynic's callousness, or even as proof of premeditation most foul. *Lucifer, knowing he could not die, made mock of all but evil*. On the other hand, Hamilton saw to it that if he fell, purity would be praised.

"To those," his *Remarks* said, "who, with me, abhorring the practise of dueling, may think that I ought on no account to have added to the number of bad examples, I answer, that my *relative* situation, as well in public as in private, enforcing all the considerations which constitute what men of the world denominate honour, imposed on me (as I thought) a peculiar necessity not to decline the call. The ability to be in future useful in resisting mischief or effecting good, in those crises of our public affairs which seem to happen, would probably be inseparable from a conformity with public prejudice in this particular." Gouverneur Morris, commenting on this, was kinder than Burr. He said it was "at the very best misguided."

Hamilton had more to say. He constructed a paragraph that has no parallel anywhere in the vast literature of the *Code Duello*. "As well because it is possible that I may have injured Colonel Burr, however convinced myself that my opinions and declarations have been well-founded, as from my general principles and temper in relation to similar affairs, I have resolved, if our interview is conducted in the usual manner, to *reserve* and *throw away* my first fire, and I *have thoughts* even of *reserving* my second fire, and thus giving a double opportunity to Colonel Burr to pause and reflect." Italics are Hamilton's. Does the wording really mean, as it is customarily capsuled, that Hamilton deliberately made himself Burr's helpless target? "If," he qualified, and "I *have thoughts*."

Should he think better of it, and shoot first and with best aim, he had only to reclaim and tear up his *Remarks*. Should he fire, but fall, his dead hand would strike from beyond the grave. Modern parlance might call it a hedged bet. No one has the right to suspect Hamilton of ignoble scheming. But reference rises in the mind, to the legendary method of vengeance known as "Chinese suicide"—according to which, if a man hates another man unbearably, he kills himself on that man's doorstep, and leaves it for the world to punish his enemy for driving him to self-destruction.

This set aside, it was in any case, by the code his *Remarks* said he must accept for honour's sake, dishonourable if not worse to place a dueling adversary in the situation Hamilton said he might impose on Burr. Gentlemen went to the Field of Honour as gamblers, staking their lives on absolutely even terms. What Hamilton did to Burr, with his posthumously published *Remarks*, was excused and in fact celebrated by his friends, because it was done by their plumed knight.

Whether that is tenable cause to brand Burr a murderer and exalt Hamilton as a martyr is open to argument. Could it conceivably have been the other way around? Is that what Burr decided to believe, after first expressing sorrow for "My friend Colonel Hamilton whom I killed"—when Hamilton's *Remarks* were used as Hamilton must have known they would be?

We have the testimony of the seconds, Van Ness and Pendleton, for what transpired at Weehawken on Wednesday, July 11, at seven in the morning. "Colonel Burr arrived first on the ground, as had been previously arranged. When General Hamilton arrived the parties exchanged salutations, and the seconds proceeded to make their arrangements. They measured the distance, ten full paces, and cast lots for the choice of position, also to determine by whom the word should be given, both of which fell to the seconds of General Hamilton."

Subsequently, claims were made that Hamilton tried both positions before choosing that which put the sun at his back, and in Burr's eyes. It was also alleged that he made much to-do of polishing and testing his spectacles to be sure his vision was unclouded. But this, like much else, was only hearsay.

The statement signed by Van Ness and Pendleton is, however, evidence entered under stipulation. The seconds "proceeded to load the pistols in each other's presence, after which the parties took their stations. The gentleman who was to give the word then explained to the parties the rules which were to govern them in firing, which were as follows: 'The parties being placed at their stations, the second who gives the word shall ask them whether they are ready; being answered in the affirmative, he shall say, *Present;* after this the parties shall present and fire when they please. If one fires before the other, the opposite second shall say *One, two, three, fire;*—and he shall then fire, or lose his fire.'

"He then asked if they were prepared; being answered in the affirmative, he gave the word, *Present,* as had been agreed on, and both parties presented and fired in succession; the intervening time is not expressed, as the seconds do not precisely agree on that point. The fire of Colonel Burr took effect, and General Hamilton almost instantly fell." Where he fell, his son, Phillip, had fallen, 30 months before.

Legend, and contemporary caricatures, have a fiendishly triumphant Burr fleeing from the scene. The seconds testified "Colonel Burr advanced to General Hamilton's friend to be expressive of regret, but without speaking turned and withdrew, being urged from the field by his friend, as has been subsequently stated, with a view to prevent his being recognized by the surgeon and barge-men, who were then approaching."

Captain Thompson, mortally wounded by William Coleman in a duel fought in Hamilton's name, with his dying breath swore all present to secrecy, lest any suffer from having taken part in an affair of honor. Not so Hamilton.

Both parties presented and fired in succession. His second, Pendleton, who loved Hamilton and hated Burr, swore to this. Dr. David Hosack, "the surgeon mutually agreed on to attend the parties," told a contradictory tale. Relating "particulars relative to the melancholy end of our beloved friend Hamilton," Dr. Hosack wrote and William Coleman published in Hamilton's New York *Evening Post:* "Soon after recovering his sight, he happened to cast his eye upon the case of pistols, and observing the one that he had had in his hand lying on the outside, he said 'Take care of that pistol; *it is undischarged, and still cocked;* it may go off and do harm;—Pendleton knows (attempting to turn his head towards him) that I did not intend to fire at him.' 'Yes,' said Mr. Pendleton, *understanding his wish,* 'I have already made Dr. Hosack acquainted with your determination as to that.'" Italics are the author's.

THE AARON BURR AFFAIR

A cross-examiner could make both witnesses squirm. But neither was ever called to give evidence under fear of perjury. A jury of Hamilton's intimates, hastily impaneled in Manhattan, heard no eyewitnesses. Legend, perpetuated by certain accepted authorities, had Burr fleeing from roused mobs, leaving New York in guilty terror. This is simply not so. He remained at Richmond Hill and went about his business until after a great funeral cortege followed Hamilton's casket to Trinity churchyard.

Even then, he left only at the insistence of worried friends, and went only as far as across the river, to visit Commodore Truxton. Devoted to Hamilton, still the doughty Commodore welcomed Burr and defended him as "having done only what any gentleman would in the circumstances."

Pendleton, along with Van Ness, declared that "The conduct of the parties in this interview was perfectly proper as suited the occasion." They were howled down. Bishop Moore said he asked the dying Hamilton, "Should it please God to restore you to health, will you employ all your influence in society to discountenance this barbarous custom (of dueling)?" and that Hamilton answered, "That, sir, is my deliberate intention."

Bishop Moore also wrote, for William Coleman in the *Evening Post*, that Hamilton "lifted up his hands and said: 'I have no ill-will against Colonel Burr. I met him with a fixed resolution to do him no harm. I forgive all that happened.'" The harm had been done, and it was not forgiven.

The Rev. Dr. Mason also told of Hamilton lifting his hands, "in the attitude of prayer," and "ejaculating 'God be merciful'; I heard not the rest distinctly, but understood him to quote the words of the publican, and to end the sentence with 'me, a sinner.'" No one begged mercy for Burr, Burr least of all.

THE AARON BURR AFFAIR

The duel, a standard reference capsules, "also killed Burr, for it made him an outcast from his country's social and political life." But that is not the whole truth. Returning to Washington, Burr served out his term as Vice President and presided over the Senate with such tact and firmness that on the day when he stepped down the Senators rose in standing ovation.

But the mark of Cain was on him and would not come off. Three years after the morning at Weehawken, he heard himself grudgingly pronounced "Not guilty" of treason and knew what the verdict was worth. Hamilton living could not drive him into outer darkness; Hamilton dying damned and doomed him. He lived on until 1836, but the Burr who might have been was slain on the Field of Honour on July 11, 1804.

WILLIAM DUER AND THE ORIGINS OF THE NEW YORK STOCK EXCHANGE

by Robert Sobel

*N*ew York in 1792 was a bustling but small city. Boys would fish off the Hudson piers at Rector Street and report large catches of lobster and crab. Collect Pond, a short walk from Chambers Street, was a favorite ice-skating place, which was reached in wintry days by sleigh rides from the Bowery. The city was dirty, as were most urban centers of the time, but the sanitation department—thirty-five scavengers and a host of pigs—did their jobs as best they could.

The pigs were kept near Bunker Hill, off Broadway near Grand Street, an area which in the summer and fall was used for bull-baiting and other manly sports. Mayor Richard Varick, an incurable optimist, looked forward to the day when the area might have to be relocated, due to the increase in the city's population. In

1792 there were some thirty-four thousand New Yorkers, few of whom lived above what is now Canal Street.

New York was one of the busiest ports in the nation, and in 1794 it would pass Philadelphia in total tonnage handled. The wharfs were fed by a good system of dirt roads and the Hudson River. Bowery Road was the major land route, with Bull's Head Tavern on Bayard Street the last stop for drovers bringing their cattle to slaughter.

Chatham Street and Broadway was New York's busiest intersection. St. Paul's Church was on one corner and a theatre and park on another. A few blocks away were a group of boarding houses used by Columbia College students, as well as by those who worked at the municipal jail, the city hospital, and the almshouse, which were also nearby.

Trinity Church, at the head of Wall Street, was a major municipal landmark, and the street itself the center of the city's business district. Alexander Hamilton had lived on Wall Street a few years earlier when the capital was in New York. City Hall was nearby—it had been used earlier as Federal Hall, the temporary seat of government—and municipal functionaries jostled with merchants and lottery ticket sellers in the several coffeehouses on the east side of the street, which ended in what was appropriately called Coffee House Wharf. The area smelled of coffee, indigo, chocolate, sugar, spices, fruits—all of which were either exported or imported by Wall Street.

The government was in Philadelphia in 1792, but former Assistant Secretary of the Treasury William Duer remained in New York. One of the social arbiters of the city, Duer kept a fine home presided over by his wife, Kitty, the daughter of Revolutionary War General Lord Sterling. A political power, Duer had arranged for the leasing of Washington's home while the President

William Duer

was in the city, had been one of those asked by Hamilton to write an essay in the *Federalist Papers* (which was not printed), and was a leading light in Federalist circles. Some thought the bright young man might one day be considered for the presidency itself!

Although interested in politics and involved in society, Duer's major interests were in business and speculation. He was in charge at Parker & Duer, Duer & Parker, and William Duer & Co., all engaged in land speculation and commerce. His name was one of those respected in London and Paris banking circles, at a time when few Americans were considered capable of large-scale business ventures. Duer would be a guiding force in the Scioto Company, a major land combine, and the Society for Useful Manufactures, the first attempt at a permanent manufacturing complex. Duer had the connections, abilities, funds, and desire to participate in speculations. A major opportunity for profit presented itself in 1792, and Duer grabbed at it with both hands.

The major speculative items in 1792 were government bonds and stock in new banks. In order to finance the new constitutional government, Secretary of the Treasury Hamilton had proposed a series of bond issues two years earlier. With Washington's aid, he was able to pursuade Congress to pass the Funding Act of 1790, which provided for the issuance of federal bonds to be exchanged for Continental and Confederate obligations.

Three types of securities were sold: six percent bonds which bore interest from the date of issue; six percents which would begin to pay interest ten years after issuance; and three percent bonds. By the end of the year, some $62 million of these bonds were sold, and the "sixes," "threes," and "six deferred" were traded both in America and Europe. In 1791 they were joined by the "B.U.S.'s." The Bank of the United

States, proposed by Hamilton, endorsed by Washington, and approved by Congress, was capitalized at $10 million (25,000 shares of $400 par value), and traded in whole, half, and quarter shares.

Although some shares were traded in Philadelphia and New York in 1791, most transactions were handled by Americans for European interests. The bonds and B.U.S. stock were hot speculative items. Since the stability of the new government was in doubt, the issues sold at a discount. Should the United States fail, they would be worthless; should the new government succeed, they would appreciate in value.

Hope & Company of Amsterdam, Daniel Crommelin & Company, with branches throughout the Netherlands, the Societé Gallo-Americaine of Paris, Etienne Clavière of Genoa, and other European houses were deep in speculation in these issues by late 1791. But they could not act intelligently without information, preferably of the "inside" variety from one with important connections. They would need American agents to handle transactions. These agents would have to be free to make decisions on the spot, and so would have to be partners, people with shares in the enterprise. William Duer filled the qualifications admirably.

As early as 1788, Parker & Duer acted as American agent for Etienne Clavière and some London firms. Van Staphorts & Hubbard and Willinks & Stadinski joined soon after. Brissot de Warville, their emissary to America, reported that Duer was one of the best speculators he had ever met. "It is difficult to unite to a great facility in calculation, more extensive views and a quicker penetration into the most complicated projects. To these qualities he joins goodness of heart; and it is to his obliging character, and his zeal, that I owe much valuable information on the finances of this country, which I shall communicate hereafter." By 1791, the combine was deep in speculation in land, bills, and, most important, government bonds and B.U.S. stock.

Speculation in government obligations, called "scrip" in the slang of the day, reached new highs in 1791. "Scripponomy," "Scriptophobia," and "Scriptomania" were terms used by conservative newspapers to describe it. "The Scriptophobia is at full height," wrote the *New York Journal and Patriotic Register;* "It has risen like a rocket—like a rocket it will burst with a crack—then down drops the rocket stick." A reader of the newspaper protested, "O that I had but cash—how soon would I have a finger in the pie!"

James Madison wrote Thomas Jefferson of the bull market, reporting that "stock and script the sole domestic subjects of conversation . . . speculations . . . carried on with money borrowed at from two and a half per cent a month to one per cent a week." And the *New York Daily Gazette* of August 13, 1791, printed one of the many poems inspired by the rush to buy securities:

SPECULATION

What magic this among the people,
That swells a may-pole to a steeple?
Touched by the wand of speculation,
A frenzy runs through all the nation;
For soon or late, so truth advises,
Things must assume their proper sizes—
And sure as death all mortal trips,
Thousands will rue the name of SCRIPTS.

Through all this, Duer reigned as king of speculators, making a reputation as well as a fortune. Then, during the last week of the year, he acted to institutionalize his new role. Meeting with Alexander Macomb, a wealthy New Yorker like himself, Duer formed what has come to be known as the "Six Per Cent Club." The two men and their partners would pool their resources to speculate in the six percent bonds and whatever other securities interested them. The Club would disband on December 31, 1792, at which time the profits would be distributed according to shares. Thus was born the first native-born American securities pool.

The Club had been formed just in time to participate in the next stage of the bull market—speculation in shares of new banks. The Tammany Bank, the Million Bank, and others were announced early in 1792, and were quickly oversubscribed. The Tammany, capitalized at $200,000 divided into 4,000 shares, received subscriptions for 21,740 shares a few hours after being first offered on January 18, and similar situations existed with other institutions. "Bancophobia" replaced scriptomania as the "in" word along Wall Street in New York and Chestnut Street in Philadelphia.

Again, the conservative newspapers were concerned, especially with the sharp rise in price for the Bank of New York. "More banks may certainly assist gambling, and enable adventurers the longer to swim on the fluctuating waves of speculation," thought a reader of the *New York Daily Advertiser*.

Alexander Hamilton was both concerned and delighted with the interest in stocks and scrip. Higher prices would mean great confidence in American securities, and this would ease his tasks in borrowing money from Europeans. On the other hand, he feared the bull market would end in a crash. Writing to William Seton, cashier of the Bank of New York, he complained of "these extravagant sallies of speculation," which "do injury to the government, and to the whole system of public credit, but disgusting all sober citizens, and giving a wild air to everything."

Hamilton realized his old friend, William Duer, was behind many of the manipulations, and he wrote to him, warning of disaster. He told Duer not to overstep himself, for this could bring ruination. "I feared lest it might carry you further than was consistent either with your own safety or the public good. My friendship for

A diorama of the first investors meeting under the Buttonwood tree at 69 Wall Street. (New York Public Library)

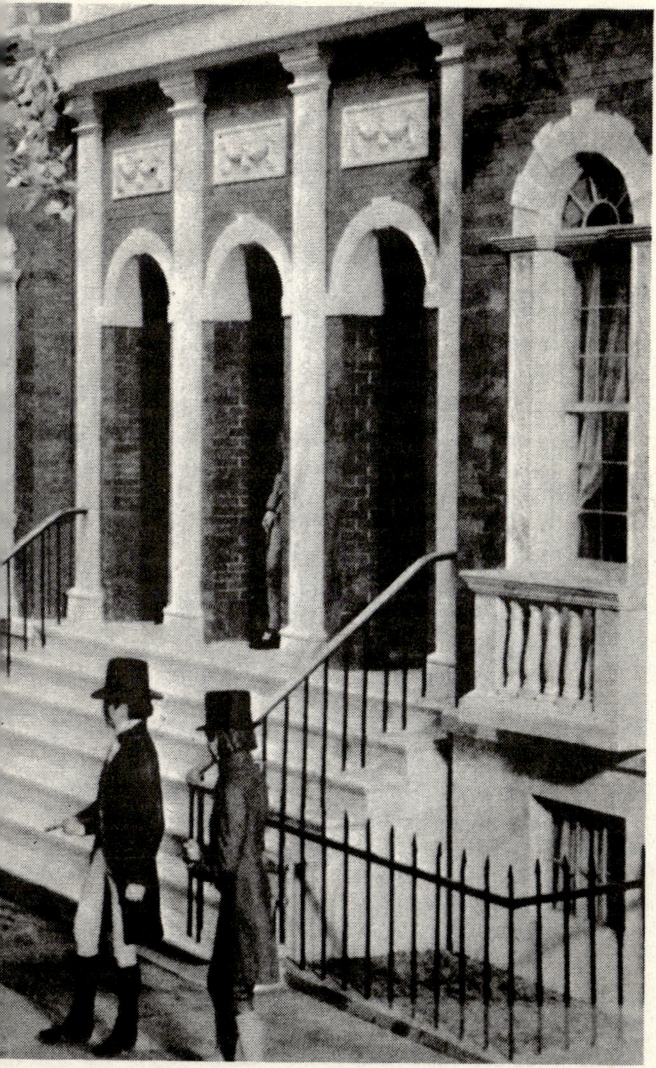

you, and my concern for the public cause, were both alarmed." But Duer continued his operations, although he assured Hamilton that all was well.

The rapid and sudden increase in securities trading created a difficult situation for those who handled such transactions. In the past, bankers, tradesmen, lottery ticket sellers, merchants, and others would handle stocks and bonds as a sideline, to be held for investment or sold if and when a good price was to be had. By early 1791, interest in securities had risen to the point where a more or less continual market was needed.

The natural place for such a market was Wall Street in New York and Chestnut Street in Philadelphia. The latter place would seem the more likely location for the large market. It was the home of the national government as well as the seat of the Bank of the United States. But it lacked a figure like William Duer, and so interest became focused on New York.

In the summer of 1791, trading took place in the street, where individuals with securities to sell would search out those who wished to buy, and vice versa. Then, as the colder weather of winter approached, the traders moved indoors, to several of the taverns along Wall Street. This created a difficulty, however. What if you wanted to buy B.U.S. stock, but no one in Merchant's Coffee House had any to sell? On the other hand, there might be a merchant or banker in another coffeehouse or tavern who wanted to sell, but had no buyer. How could the two be brought together? Clearly, a central market was badly needed.

Attempts were made that winter to solve this problem. Commodities such as sugar and tobacco were bought and sold at auctions. Why not have similar auctions for stocks and bonds? Several appeared in the latter part of 1791, and they advertised in the many New York papers their locations and times.

Usually, the auctions were held shortly after the midday meal. Sellers would deposit their securities with the auctioneer, who would then call them off for the buyers. Most transactions were made on time, with money and security exchanged sixty days after the contract was made. By early 1792 there were a dozen or so such auctions in the city, most of them around Wall Street, and some auctioneers were so busy that they had to schedule two sessions, one in the morning, the other in the afternoon.

The system created more problems than it solved. In the first place, the auctions were held at the same time, and the potential buyer and seller might be at different locations—as had been the case earlier—and the transaction lost. But more important, the new system placed both buyer and seller at the mercy of the auctioneers, who had formed a guild-like combine to periodically raise their fees. Clearly such a situation could not be tolerated.

On March 11, 1792, the following advertisement appeared in *Louden's Register* and other newspapers: "The Stock Exchange office is opened at No. 22 Wall Street for the accommodation of the dealers in Stock, and in which Public Sales will be held daily at noon as usual in rotation by A. L. Bleeker & Sons, J. Pintard, McEvers and Barclay, Cortland & Ferrers, and Jay & Sutton."

These firms, leading brokers all, had combined their forces to combat the auctioneers. From that time on, they would hold their own auction and do away with the hated commissions. Considering the size of their auction, they believed it would soon put the others out of business.

The new auction was an immediate success, and the participants next considered putting their association into a more permanent form. On May 17, they gathered at Corre's Hotel and signed an agreement which established what amounted to a brokers' guild: "We, the subscribers, brokers for the purchase and sale of public stocks, do hereby solemnly promise and pledge ourselves to each other that we will not buy or sell from this date, for any person whatsoever, any kind of public stocks at a less rate than one-quarter of one per cent commission on the specie value, and that we will give preference to each other in our negotiations." The Corre's Hotel Pact is usually considered the basic document which organized the New York Stock Exchange.

Soon after, the brokers decided to build their own coffeehouse and exchange. A Subscription for 203 shares of stock at $200 a share was quickly raised, the money used to buy land and construct the Tontine Coffee House at the corner of Wall and Water streets.

The Pact and the Tontine would not have been possible were it not for William Duer. It was Duer who made a securities market necessary by sparking the investment and speculation bull market of 1792, and it was Duer who made New York, and not Philadelphia, the central city of American securities. But Duer did not sign the Corre's Hotel Pact, nor was he a member of the Tontine. By then, he was otherwise occupied.

As buyers and sellers rushed to and fro from auctions in March, William Duer would sit in his Wall Street office, ordering purchases and sales, organizing new ventures, and in general building what he hoped would become a major fortune. By early March, Duer was playing both sides of the market at the same time. He would buy in conjunction with one syndicate, and sell with another. Since he controlled both groups, he would act in such a way as to maximize his gains. Never before or since has a single individual exercised so much control over the market. Perhaps this was the reason that Duer lost his head.

By the second week in March, he started to believe his own propaganda, and was convinced the market

WILLIAM DUER AND THE STOCK EXCHANGE

would rise indefinitely. Accordingly, he plunged in on the bull side, signing several large purchase orders for bank stock. The money would not be payable for several days, and by then, thought Duer, the stock prices will have risen so high that he would have a handsome profit without having committed a cent.

But prices did not rise; instead they leveled off, and then started to decline, crowding the auctions with worried sellers and a few hopeful buyers. On March 6, the six percents had sold for 24 shillings, 4 pence; by March 15, the price had fallen to 21 shillings, 4 pence, and other issues fell similar amounts. Money dried up on Wall Street and elsewhere, and Duer was unable to borrow funds to cover his debts.

At the same time, discrepancies were uncovered in his accounts. Comptroller of the Treasury Oliver Wolcott informed Duer that he owed the government almost a quarter of a million dollars from the time he was Assistant Secretary of Treasury.

Duer ran from one friend to another, contacting all his associates, with no luck; he could not raise money for either his shortages or his stock contracts. In desperation, he wrote to Hamilton, pleading for aid. But before an answer would arrive in New York, Duer was finished. "I am now secure from my enemies, and feeling the purity of my heart defy the world." Thus, Duer assured an associate, Walter Livingston, that all was well. It was March 22. Within twenty-four hours, the master speculator would be taken to debtors' prison.

The next week saw the first major financial panic in American history, an event for which the brokers' auction at No. 22 Wall Street had not been prepared. The office was jammed with sellers and individuals, seeking credit or loans. John Pintard, a founder of the auction and one of the city's leading figures, was also involved in speculation; he fled to New Jersey. The leader of one of New York's first families, Walter Livingston, ran

Wall Street soon after the Stock Exchange was founded in 1792. (New York Stock Exchange)

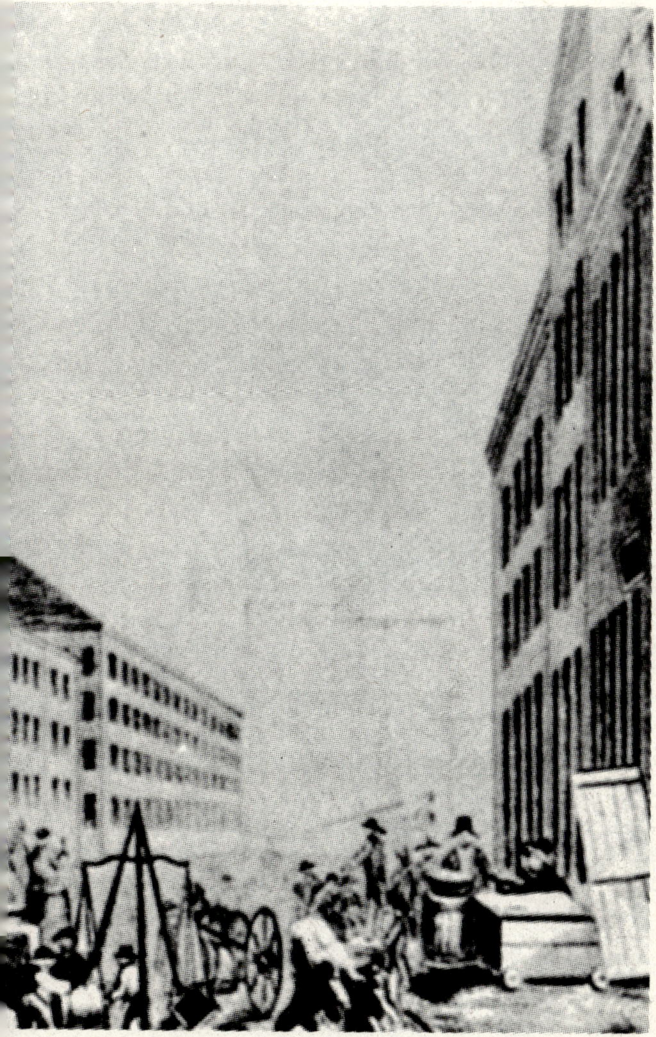

from door to door declaring his solvency.

Pierre de Peyster was more realistic. He owned a Duer note and meant to collect. He ran to the prison, and confronted Duer with a brace of dueling pistols. Pay me now, he cried, or be prepared to defend your honor! Duer paid de Peyster $1,500, and the challenger left.

The panic was short-lived, ending when Hamilton threw his resources of the Treasury behind selected government issues. As the brokers met in Corre's Hotel that May prosperity had returned. The *National Gazette* reported that there were few signs of the March disaster left. "The shock of the time was very severe, but of short continuance." Stocks were rising, "credit is again revived—and prosperity once more approaches in sight." Pintard was back in the city, and a wiser Livingston again was looking for investments. Duer was in jail, where he would remain until his death on May 7, 1799.

It snowed on January 1, 1793, and the skaters at Collect Pond were obliged to return to their homes. Ice formed on the Hudson, and small boys cut holes and poked their lines into the frigid water, searching for fish. Jefferson had estimated that more than $5 million had been wiped out in the panic, but there were no signs of it that day. On the surface at least, the city was the same as it had been a year earlier when Duer formed the Six Per Cent Club. But there was one major difference. The cornerstone had been laid for the Tontine Coffee House, the first home of the New York Stock Exchange, which was made possible by William Duer, and remains his most significant contribution.

JOHN ADAMS THE FIRST ANGRY MAN IN THE WHITE HOUSE

by Robert Hardy Andrews

I must study politics and war that my sons may have liberty to study mathematics and philosophy.

The more young people know of the cause of revolutions, the more they will detest that ruinous policy which holds that it is useful to be unjust, deceitful, and wicked.

The political and literary world are much indebted for the invention of the new word IDEOLOGY. And a very profound, abstruse, and mysterious science it is. You must descend deeper than the divers in the Dunciad to make any discoveries, and after that you will find no bottom. It is the bathos, the theory, the art, the skill, of diving and sinking in government.

I begin to think that learned academies, not under the immediate inspection and control of government, have disorganized the world, and are incompatible with social order.

I will not bear the Reproaches of my Children.—I will tell them that I studied and laboured to procure a free Constitution of Government for them to Solace themselves under, and if they do not prefer this to ample Fortune, to Ease & Elegance, and will if needs must live on thin air, wear mean clothes, and work hard, so that freedom may be theirs and their childrens', then they are not my children and I care not what becomes of them!

—From the jottings of John Adams
1735-1826

He was, he said without self-pity but rather with pawky pride, "obnoxious, suspected, and unpopular." He stepped up from Vice President to President thanking no one but himself for achievement of his heart's desire, declaring at the start: "I have taken office with a sense of grievance and suspicion." During his single elected term, he managed matters in such ways that no one argued when with the next election impending he announced: "I am abjured and abhorred by all parties." He left the White House ungraciously, his leaving mourned by no one, and retired to his farm proclaiming: "For fifty years, I have constantly lived in an enemies' country." He spoke stark truth when he summarized his half-century in politics: "I could never do anything but what was ascribed to sinister motives." A man whose personal gospel was always "I am always right," he was never as correct as when he prophesied: "Mausoleums, statues, monuments, will never be erected to me. Panegyrical romances will never be written, nor flattering orations spoken to transmit me to posterity in brilliant colours." And he brought this on himself.

He was pompous, vain, self-righteous, envious, vehement, tactless, too openly ambitious, too frankly contemptuous of the crowd, needlessly acerbate in personal relations—all things a political professional cannot afford to be and a lonely soul who longs to be liked (as he longed secretly) must not be if he hopes tears will be shed at his funeral. He was also, as a Frenchman wrote when his countrymen thought otherwise, "a man of merits, ability, and culture rarely equaled in America," and as the record will show, a giant among the Founding Fathers.

He was crusty, cranky John Adams, first Vice President and second President of the United States, first to occupy the White House, more generally if least excusably rejected as a candidate for reelection than any incumbent since. A farmer's son, born near Quincy, Massachusetts, in 1735, he graduated from Harvard at 20, taught school while learning law, and at 23 was admitted to the bar.

Samuel Adams, his second cousin, 13 years his senior, had failed in business, failed even as a tax-collector, but was notably successful at winning friends and influencing people. Young John, contrarily, accumulated ill-wishers as rapidly as he rose in his profession. From the first he jotted down impressions of prominent persons, which he quoted wherever there was an audience. In open court he called a rival lawyer "a numskull and a blunderbuss," capsuled another as "a very sagacious trifler," and dismissed a third with "I will not waste my time in listening to his feeble effeminate voice."

Meanwhile he joined the strengthening underground movement against British policies, and was grudgingly accepted "because Sam Adams is his cousin." Sam Adams organized Boston merchants in a boycott of British imports. The Stamp Act raised a cry of "taxation without representation." Two British regiments marched into Boston and camped on the Common when citizens refused to provide billets.

On March 5, 1770, protest demonstrators, mostly youths out for fun and frolic, confronted a red-coated sentry posted on King Street (now State Street). He summoned his officer and a squad of musketeers. Denounced as rebels and commanded to disperse, the Bostonians stood firm. The British opened fire, killing four unarmed civilians (some authorities say five). Among the dead was Crispus Attucks, then and since variously described as a mulatto or of mixed Negro and Indian blood, in any event justly honored as the first American of his color to die in the cause of freedom.

The Boston Massacre made martyrs, which made future rebellion inevitable. Its immediate effect was such anger spreading across the Colonies that when Sam Adams demanded immediate withdrawal of the British regiments the British governor offered placating compromise. Rejecting his proposal to send one regiment out of the city, Sam Adams said, "Both or none." Further, the officers and soldiers held responsible for the shooting must stand trial on murder indictments. The governor temporized. Bostonians swarmed in the streets, and riders came in from up and down New England. The governor gave in. Then John Adams stunned his cousin, shocked Boston, and in the pleased opinion of his foes committed professional suicide by volunteering to defend the sacrificial scapegoats "because passion and prejudice are not admissible in a court of law."

He was a year married to Abigail Smith, the gently wise and quietly militant daughter of a Congregational minister, when he jotted in his private papers in 1765: "Let us dare to read, think, speak, and write. Let the public disputations become researches into the grounds and nature and ends of government, and the means of preserving the good and demolishing the evil." In 1770, their first-born son, John Quincy Adams, was a child of three. (In 1825, while his father still lived, he

John Adams

became the sixth President of the United States.) The family was settled at Quincy. He was enlarging his farm, adding to his house, beginning collection of the largest and most comprehensive library owned by any American in his times. He had nothing but more unpopularity to earn by espousing a case in which the verdict was foregone. But he plunged into it headlong.

Against the odds, he won. On strict legalities, the officer and most of his men were acquitted. Only two were found guilty—of manslaughter. They were branded on the hand and released. Their rescuer collected no fee. But the same proper Bostonians who had accused him of "un-American sympathies" told each other, "I don't have to like a man to hire him when I need a lawyer." Sam Adams organized the Boston Tea Party. John Adams practiced prosperously, played no politics, but showed no surprise when he was delegated to go along with Cousin Sam to the First Continental Congress in 1774. There Sam was happily at home among politicians. Cousin John jotted in a moment of self-appraisal: "I have insensibly fallen into a habit of affecting wit and humour; of shrugging my shoulders and moving and distorting the muscles of my face"—which seems to have meant he tried to imitate Cousin Sam. But not for long. "My motions are stiff and uneasy, ungraceful; and my attention is unsteady and irregular." He went back to being the real John Adams.

In 1775, he judged that "At least a third of the two million and some people now living in the thirteen Colonies are opposed to the Revolution, and to the whole idea of Independence." The practical-minded delegates—whom he dubbed, not as a compliment, the Cool Considerates—talked on and on. "Nothing was said today, nothing is likely to be said tomorrow or the day after or the day after that, but what has already been repeated and hackneyed a hundred times before. All the gentlemen in the Congress want is delay, delay;

Abigail Adams

thus only they hope to defeat us, and thus they will defeat us if they can."

His "us" was closer to "me." Seconding the nomination of George Washington as commander-in-chief, he did so as if he alone saw the right and set example to be followed. Subsequently, he confided to Dr. Benjamin Rush: "The history of our Revolution will be that Benjamin Franklin's electrical rod smote the earth and out sprang General Washington. That Dr. Franklin electrified him with his rod, and thence forward these two conducted all the policy, negotiations, legislatures, and war." He stood on evidence to the contrary.

On the morning of May 15, 1776, he demanded the floor, and began to read in a loud voice a *Preamble and Resolve* over which he had labored while Cousin Sam was busy in cloakroom caucuses. "For the preservation of internal peace, virtue, and good order, as well as for the defense of their lives, liberties, and properties, against the hostile invasions and cruel depredations of their enemies . . ."

William Duane, a delegate from New York, leaped to his feet protesting. Duane was a firebrand by trade, a warrior with his pen who had been deported from India to England for criticizing colonial policy in the East, and from England to America for criticizing policy toward the Colonies. But now he shouted: "Congress has no right to pass on such a *Preamble!* It is a mechanism for the fabrication of Independence! As such I do protest it!"

A gavel pounded until silence fell. Then it was realized that John Adams had gone on reading during the disturbance. He finished and seemed unsurprised when his *Preamble* was adopted as written. Duane pushed toward him, crying "Adams, you are aware, I presume, of what you have done? You have created a machine for the fabrication of Independence!" The answer was not to Duane, but to all present, and they might like it

John Quincy Adams

or lump it. "Not a mere machine, Duane. This is Independence itself." By unanimous vote, the Congress recessed on May 17, declaring "A Day of Fasting and Prayer." There had been a day of fasting and prayer after Lexington, and another after Bunker Hill. It was Friday, but John Adams and Cousin Sam and 50 other delegates went to church in a body.

At sunrise next morning, a letter went off to Abigail Adams at home in Massachusetts. "Is it not a saying of Moses—who am I, that I should go in and out before this great People?—When I consider the great Events which are passed and those greater which are rapidly advancing, and that I may have been instrumental of touching some Springs and turning some Small Wheels, which have had and will have such Effects, I feel an Awe upon my Mind which is not easily described."

To William Cushing: "Objects of the most stupendous magnitude, and measures in which the lives and liberties of millions yet unborn are intimately interested, are now before us. We are in the midst of a revolution, the most complete, unexpected, and remarkable, of any in the history of nations." What about objectors to his *Preamble*? "You can't make thirteen Clocks strike precisely alike, no matter how you set them." What if he failed? "I will petition my constituents to let me go home. I will live with my family, practice law, make money, and be at peace."

On June 4, 1776, Washington left the capital at Philadelphia to resume command of the Continental Army. Departing, he expressed frank doubt that he could hold his forces together or continue the war, "unless some great decision in Congress gives new spirit to the soldiers and to their families at home." On June 7, Richard Henry Lee of Virginia rose to offer a *Resolution*. The night before, Sam Adams had written to Massachusetts: "Tomorrow a Motion will be made, and a Question I hope decided, the most important ever agi-

George Washington

tated in America." The motion was *"Resolved,* that these United Colonies are, and of right ought to be, totally dissolved."

Debate next day was loud and long, and led nowhere. Finally, on June 10, those opposed to the shocking thought of independence obtained a vote postponing action on Lee's *Resolution* until July 1. By then the British Expeditionary Force was expected to reach New York. The Cool Considerates expected its arrival to silence even John Adams. But he buzzed and bullied, and gained a token concession—that a committee might discuss "some sort of a Declaration," so no time would be lost in the highly unlikely event that the Congress might still pass Lee's *Resolution.*

"The members chosen are Mr. Jefferson, Mr. J. Adams, Mr. Franklin, Mr. Sherman, Mr. R. R. Livingston." Of the five, the least known and least expected to go far was Thomas Jefferson, then only 33. According to John Adams: "During the whole time I have sat with Jefferson in Congress, I have never heard him utter more than three words together in any public discussion." Benjamin Franklin was the great man of the committee, as of Congress. Robert R. Livingston, only 30, had for ten years been New York's highest-paid attorney. Roger Sherman, from Connecticut, was a lank, farmer-looking zealot, who made no secret of his conviction that Jefferson and Adams were reckless radicals, and he meant to keep them in check or know the reason why not.

John Adams noted in his day-book: "Jefferson is chairman because he had most votes; and he had most votes because we were united to keep out Richard Henry Lee." Later, he told it differently. "The question arose as to who, as our chairman, should write the general statement of philosophy with which we should preface our *Bill of Particulars* as to the injuries and usurpations the Colonies had suffered. We wished it to be clear to all the world that our rebellion had been undertaken not in anger, but in defense of the rights of man.

"Mr. Jefferson proposed that I should make the draft. I said 'I will not.' He said 'You should.' 'Oh, no!' I answered. 'Why not?' he asked. 'Reason enough,' I told him. 'You must write it, not I.' He asked then: 'What can be your reasons?' I replied: 'Reason first—you are a Virginian, and a Virginian ought to appear at the head of this business. Reason second—I am obnoxious, suspected, and unpopular. You are very much otherwise. Reason third—you can write ten times better than I can.' 'Well,' said Jefferson, 'if you are decided, I will do as well as I can.'" How well that was is history.

"During the work of preparing the Declaration," Adams testified *post-facto*, "I was shunned like a man infected with the leprosy; I walked the streets of Philadelphia in solitude, borne by the weight of care and unpopularity." The night of June 12, from Byrne's Tavern on Race Street near the Common, he wrote to Francis Dana, member of the Massachusetts Council: "We are drudging on, as usual. Sometimes it is 7 o'clock before we finish. We have greater Things in Contemplation than ever—the greatest of all which we shall ever have. Be silent and patient, and time will bring forth, after the usual Groans, Throes, and Pains upon such Occasions, a fine vigorous, healthy Boy, I presume. God bless him, and make him a great wise virtuous, rich and powerful and pious Full Man!"

On June 29, the British Expeditionary armada was sighted off Sandy Hook. "A fleet of 130 sail," Congress was told. Actually there were 52 warships, 27 armed sloops and cutters, and nearly 400 troop transports. "If Washington's little army shall be driven across the Hudson River, into New Jersey or Pennsylvania, the war may last 15 years, or may be over and lost in a week."

The State House in Boston was the colonial capitol. (Library of Congress)

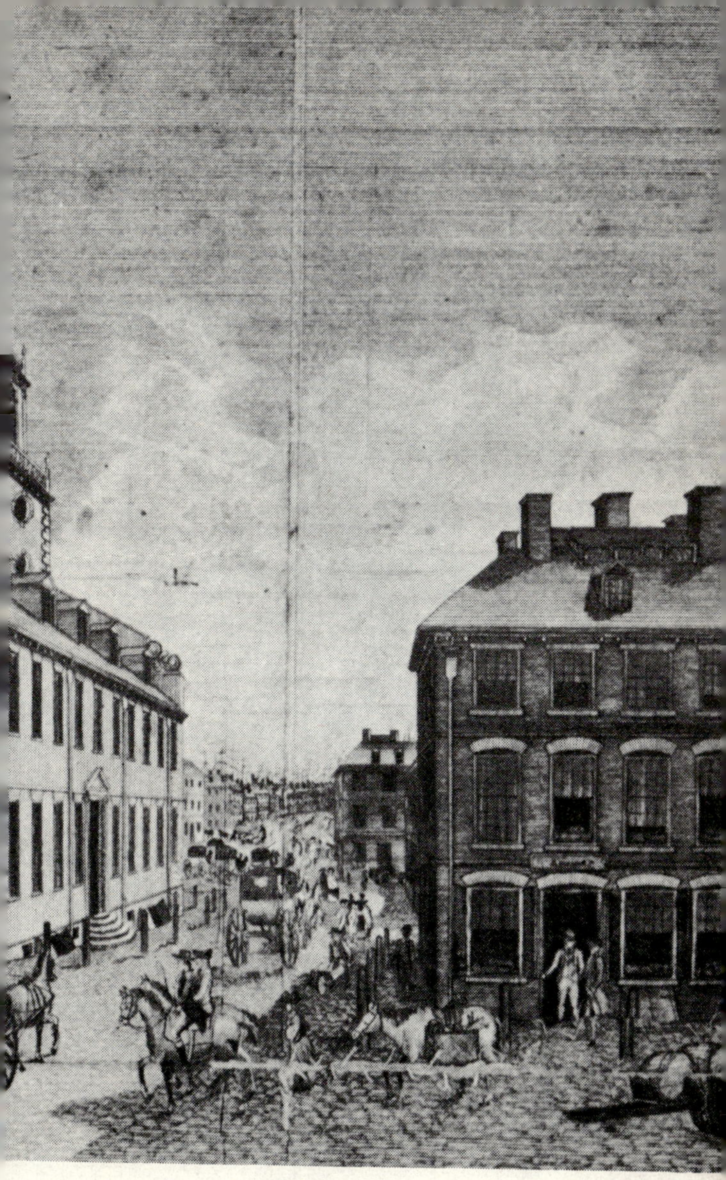

"Give me liberty or give me death!" shouted Patrick Henry at the Virginia Provincial Convention in 1775.
(Library of Congress)

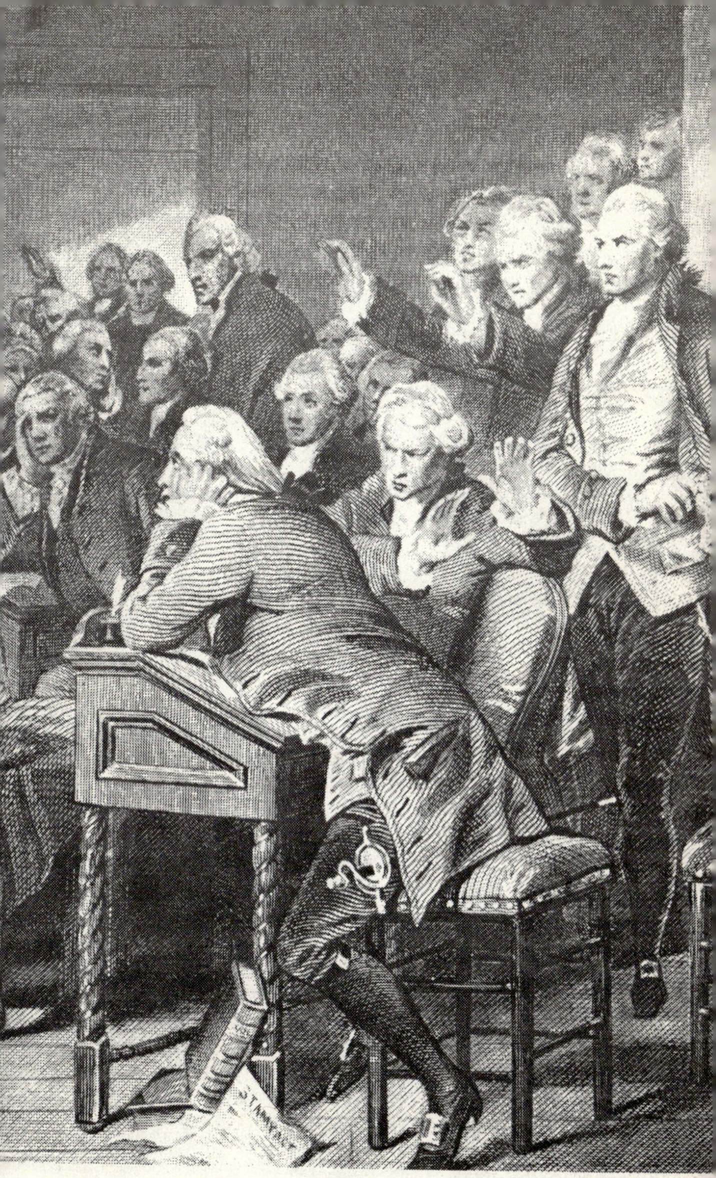

"Declaration of Independence" mural by Barry Faulkner.
(Library of Congress)

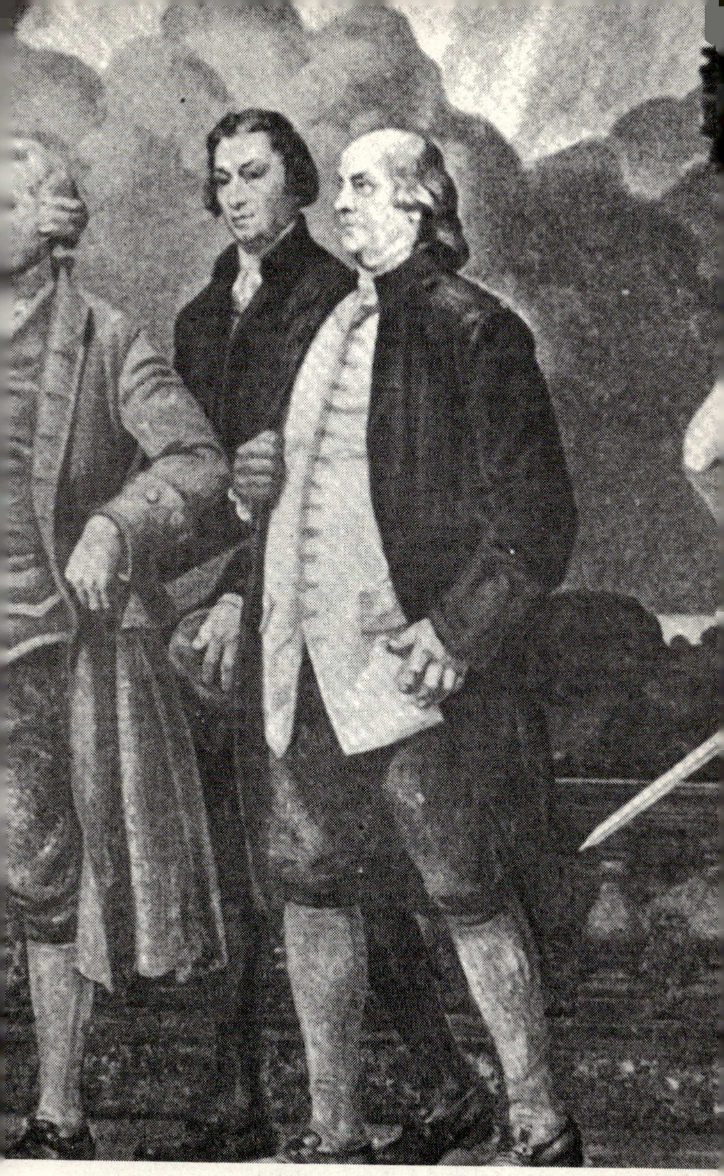

On July 1, six weeks after Adams introduced his *Preamble and Resolve*, voting began on Lee's *Resolution*. Unless this passed, the *Declaration* would never be seen by any but the five who had prepared it. Jefferson had done the writing. Adams led the vote-getting. Slightly revised the *Declaration* was approved late on July 4. But John Adams died insisting that the true Independence Day was July 2, when Lee's *Resolution*, the child of his *Preamble*, was passed, thus making the *Declaration*—in his estimation—only an implementing document.

"Yesterday, July 2nd," he wrote to Abigail, "the greatest question was decided, that was ever decided in America; and a greater, perhaps, never was nor will be decided among men. The 2nd day of July will be the most memorable epoch in the history of America. I am apt to believe that it will be celebrated by succeeding generations as the day of deliverance, by solemn acts of devotion to God Almighty." Wrong by two days, he continued to err just sufficiently to keep him in second place. In 1778, he went to France as member of a commission he was not permitted to head. In 1779, although officially he ranked as minister plenipotentiary, he was instructed to take orders from Franklin. The chip on his shoulder grew taller.

In 1787, he published his bid for highest office, *A Defence of the Constitutions of Government of the United States*. It proposed a Senate restricted to "the rich; the well-born and the able," modeled on the British House of Lords. There was a roar of "monarchist!" He stuck to his guns. "The fundamental article of my political creed is that despotism, or unlimited sovereignty, or absolute power, is the same in a majority of a popular assembly, an aristocratical council, an oligarchical junto, and a single emperor. The majority may be omnipotent, but it is not omniscient."

Delightedly, his enemies agreed: "He is verifying

completely the last feature in the character drawn of him by Dr. Franklin, however his title may stand to the two first, 'Always an honest man, often a wise one, but sometimes, in some things, wholly out of his senses.'" To their surprise, he found a following that placed him on the ticket with Washington in the first Presidential election. Property qualifications and, in some areas, religious affiliation, restricted the franchise to fewer than one in 20 citizens. Legislatures named Presidential electors. As yet, there were no party designations. Electors cast first- and second-choice ballots.

Recklessly, Adams questioned the Olympian greatness of the Father of His Country. "The history of our Revolution will be one continued lie from one end to the other. The essence of the whole will be that Dr. Franklin's electrical rod smote the earth and out sprang General Washington. That Franklin electrified him with his rod—and thence forward these two conducted all the policy, negotiations, legislation, and war." Instead of winning votes, this lost some that he might have had. Washington was the unanimous first choice. Adams received only 34 second-choice votes. "My country," he wrote bitterly to Abigail, "has in its wisdom consigned me to the most insignificant office that ever the invention of man contrived." He took office as Vice President "with a sense of grievance and of suspicion of many of the leading men."

Presiding over the Senate, he pushed through a measure under which the President would be addressed as "His Highness the President of the United States and Protector of the Rights of Same." Jefferson called this "the most superlatively ridiculous thing I ever heard of." Unkinder critics said Adams promoted "His Highness" only because he hoped to inherit the crown and dubbed him "His Rotundity." His defense of British soldiers after the Boston Massacre, his book proposing an American House of Lords, his effort to royalize the

Chief Executive, were cited as proof that he headed "an American faction of Anglican monarchists."

Unquestionably there was such a faction. Its leaders had talked of forcing Washington to accept a crown. Jefferson neither avowed nor disavowed a letter ascribed to him, widely circulated in Europe, that said: "It would give you a fever were I to name the apostates who have gone over to these heresies, men who were Samsons in the field and Solomons in the Council, but who have had their heads shorn by the harlot England." The House of Representatives killed the "Highness" bill almost by acclamation. But then along came Thomas Paine, whose *Common Sense* had made him a hero during times that tried men's souls. Now Paine brought out *The Rights of Man*, defending extremism in the French Revolution and calling on the British to emulate their American cousins and their neighbors across the Channel by overthrowing their kind and founding a republic.

Adams made no secret of his approval of articles signed *Publicola*, which excoriated excesses in France and Paine for praising them. Word spread that *Publicola* was his son, John Quincy, now 21, at 14 the private secretary to the first American envoy to Russia, educated in Paris and at the University of Leyden, his father's pride and joy. Adams was denounced for using his son as a shield. Still no cabal would remove him from the succession.

Forced out of Washington's Cabinet when he challenged Alexander Hamilton's right, as first Secretary of the Treasury, to usurp his functions as first Secretary of State, Jefferson plunged into formation of this first opposition. Washington—serving his second term as President with Adams as Vice President—"relegated," Adams was sure by now, "to what must be perpetual obscurity"—was shocked when he learned what was happening. "Self-created political societies," he warned, might have to be put down by the government. The result made him the first President to fall from acclaim to obloquy within five years.

"I have been blackened and villified," he protested wonderingly, "in such terms as could scarcely be applied to a common pickpocket." In a Cabinet meeting, Jefferson said: "General Washington declared he would rather be in his grave than in his present situation; that he had rather be on his farm than be made Emperor of the World!" And in 1796, he refused to serve longer, and went home to Mount Vernon to die. At long last, Adams was first choice. Yet, before he took his oath "to defend and perpetuate the United States," he snorted privately: "There never was a democracy that did not commit suicide." His enemies sniggered that this was because, in return for his election, he was forced to accept a Cabinet which—he wailed—reported to Alexander Hamilton, not him.

The ruling Establishment was now called Federalist, and Hamilton was its ruler. Friction between the United States and France had brought on undeclared war at sea. The toll was killing New England's export trade, closing banks, driving merchants to the wall. Hamilton appealed for a new army "for defense against radicals." Washington, named commander-in-chief, gave Hamilton actual command. In Paris, Hamilton's confidant, Charles Cotesworth Pinckney, rejected contemptuous offers to accept a bribe in return for peace. "Millions for defense, but not one cent for tribute!" Most Americans cheered. Not so Adams. The Jeffersonians cried, "We will keep you out of war!" Hamilton notwithstanding, so did the angry man in the White House.

"The situation is such," Jefferson wrote to James Madison, "that 250 votes one way or the other may set the course of history in the United States for the next 100 years." Burr delivered the winning margin. Gleefully, Madison wrote from Philadelphia, then still the national capital: "The Federalists have been so long accustomed to conquer, and the Republicans to be only a vehement, despised and hopeless opposition, that the probability of the two parties exchanging positions produces an effect like that of a volcano about to erupt. All eyes naturally go to Mr. Jefferson, as the man destined to wield the power of patronage of the government." (It should be noted that although at the time his followers called themselves Republicans, what Jefferson had founded was to become the Democratic Party.)

Jefferson recorded: "On the day when we learned the New York vote, which will determine the vote of the Union, I called on President Adams. He was very sensibly affected by the news, and accosted me with these words: 'Well, I understand that you are to beat me, and I will only say that I will be as faithful a subject as any you will have.' 'Mr. Adams,' I said, 'this is no contest between you and me. Two systems of principles, on the subject of government, divide our fellow-citizens. One of these parties has put you at its head; the other has named me. Were we both to die today, tomorrow two other names would be in place of ours, without any change in the motion of the machinery.' 'I believe you are right,' said he, 'that we are but passive instruments, and should not suffer this matter to affect our personal dispositions.'"

Canard enhallowed by legend, and stated as fact in some political histories, has it that to the day of their death, Adams and Hamilton were mortal enemies. The contrary is true. The adversary Adams hated was Alexander Hamilton, who at this stage wrote to his intimates, "My mind is made up. I will never again be responsible to Adams by my direct support."

In his journal, Adams noted: "Walking in the streets of Philadelphia, I met Colonel Joseph Lyman, one of the most amiable men in Congress. He said 'Sir, I cross over to give you some news.' 'Ay? What news? I hope it is good.' 'Hamilton is going to divide the Federalists, and give you the go-by.' 'How can that be?' 'He has a plan, and will pursue it, though I am sure it will give offense to the honester part of the party. In the long run, it will be the ruin of Hamilton and his faction.' My answer was: 'It may be, as you say, the ruin of Hamilton and his faction. But the tragedy is, it will also ruin honester men than any of them.' And I walked on my way." He went on walking his way as he always had, lonely as he had always been, still baffled by the fate that robbed him of ability "to appeal to the imaginations and affections of the people as a whole," one of "few men in American history who have, during their lifetime, been regarded with so much hostility and attacked with so much rancour."

On August 1, 1800, Hamilton received from a printer sworn to secrecy copies of the most explosive pamphlet ever issued during a Presidential campaign. Headed *A Letter From Alexander Hamilton, Concerning the Public Conduct and Private Character of John Adams, Esquire, President of the United States*, and intended for confidential circulation first in New England, then in the Deep South so late in the campaign that news of it could never get back to the North until voting there was over, the *Letter* poured invective on Adams, denouncing him for "extreme egotism of temper," and as being "unfit for the office of Chief Magistrate." The plan it presented was that *pro forma* Adams and Pinckney would be supported as candidates respectively for President and Vice President, but that Pinckney would be given a few more votes than Adams, and thus elected President. Adams, thrust back into second place, could be counted on to resign.

The scheme might have worked, but for Burr, who obtained a copy of the *Letter* and immediately published it. "This produced all the effect the bitterest enemy of the Federalist party could desire. Astonish-

In this contemporary cartoon the horse (America) is shown throwing George III off its back. (Library of Congress)

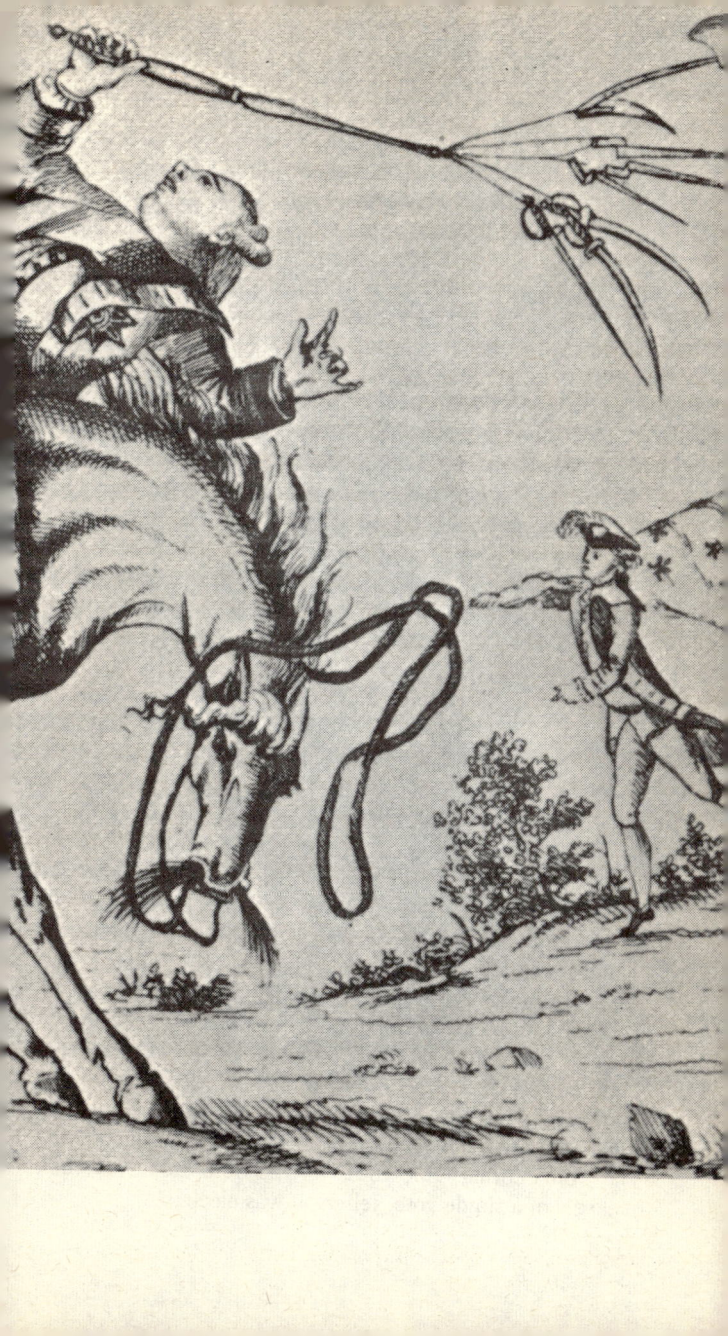

ment and incredulity beset the Federalist intellect." William Duane wrote to a friend in France: "This has done more mischief to the parties concerned than all that has gone before." John Adams jotted with his pen scratching through the page: "If the single purpose had been to defeat the President, no more propitious moment could have been chosen. One thing I know, that Cicero was not sacrificed to the vengeance of Antony, by unfeeling selfishness, more egregiously than John Adams was to the unbridled ambition of that bastard son of a Scots peddler, Alexander Hamilton."

It had never happened before, and fortunately, it has not happened since. The electoral vote was 75 for Jefferson, 75 for Burr, with Adams a distant third. Decision rested with the House of Representatives, where voting began on February 11, 1801. As the Constitution then provided, Congressmen must vote by states, with a majority—nine out of 16 then comprising the Union—required to elect. One hundred and six Representatives must choose between Jefferson and Burr. Balloting could not be—as many wished it was—in secret. Sergeants-at-arms compelled all to be present, with sofas provided for those too ill to sit up. One Congressman was carried in on a stretcher, attended by his weeping wife, who gave him medicine now and then, meanwhile praying loudly for the benighted nation now being punished for its sins. Senators attended in a body, but were not permitted to offer comments or suggestions. They sat in the gallery. John Adams sat apart from them. The public was excluded.

Balloting went on for days. The governors of Virginia and Pennsylvania called out their militia. There was talk of secession. Federalists in several cities urged an emergency law making the Chief Justice of the Supreme Court "the temporary ruler of the country." At last, on February 17, 1801, on the 36th ballot, by the margin of a single vote, Jefferson was elected.

After half a century, his country had no more use for John Adams. In his last hours of power, he scribbled furiously, piling up appointments to the Federal bench, creating the so-called "Midnight Judges" to serve until removed by death or impeachment. They could be counted on to invoke the Constitution against radicalism as he defined that misused word. Again, the obnoxious, suspected, and unpopular architect of so much for which no one would give him credit was damned for a good deed. For among his appointment in the final hour was one that gave the country its most honored Chief Justice, John Marshall.

John Adams had 26 years to live. In 1818, after long illness, Abigail Adams died, and he was left with only his books for company. In 1822, he gave the books to the library in Quincy. There were 3,000 volumes. In more than a hundred of them, he had jotted marginal notes, some of which were only sentences, while many were commentaries running to 4,000 words. Two were each 12,000 words long. In all, he argued with the authors. "How sincerely this fellow lies!" recurred in numerous places. In ten months in his 82nd year, he read 43 thick treatises, some in Greek or Latin, a number in French. "And to what purpose? I verily believe I was as wise and good 70 years ago as I am now." In 1823, feeble, nearly blind, "scarcely able to walk across a room without assistance," he sat up straight, jaw set, head held high, for his portrait by Gilbert Stuart, who was also growing old.

He said, and meant, "I always loved Jefferson, and still love him." Hearing this, Jefferson wrote to Dr. Benjamin Rush, who made himself their intermediary: "I only needed this knowledge to revive toward him all the affections of the most cordial moments of our lives." From then on, their correspondence was uninterrupted. In 1826, Jefferson wrote for the last time, "Beset with difficulties and dangers, we were fellow-labourers in the same cause, struggling for what is most valuable to man, his right of self-government. Labouring always at the same oar, with some wave ever ahead threatening to overwhelm us, and yet passing harmless under our bark, we knew not how we rode through the storm with heart and hand, and made a happy port . . . And so we have gone on and on, and so we shall go on, puzzled and prospering beyond example in the history of men."

On July 9, 1826, racing from Washington by four-horse coach, John Quincy Adams learned that his father had died five days before, near the end of his 91st year. The same day, in nearly the same hour, Jefferson died asking for no epitaph beyond "Author of the Declaration of Independence." Only a few knew that in his final moments John Adams renounced his proudest claim, that he, not Jefferson, was the author of independence and that its anniversary should be celebrated on July 2. "This is," he whispered, "a great day. It is a good day." Then with his last breath, the man who wanted always to be first accepted second place. In the moment of death, John Adams said: "Thomas Jefferson survives."

THE RIDE A NATION FORGOT

by **Howald Bailey**

Visitors to Monticello, Thomas Jefferson's beautiful mansion just three miles east of Charlottesville, Virginia, are often puzzled by a bronze star they see imbedded in one of the steps leading up to the front portico of our third President's mansion. It is a modest star, perhaps no more than five inches from point to point, but it symbolizes a heroic yet little-known Revolutionary War episode that undoubtedly changed the course of American history.

Guides at Monticello will explain to the inquisitive visitor that this star marks the exact spot where a Virginia militiaman—Captain Jack Jouett—halted his exhausted horse after a 40-mile, night-long dash through rough backwoods country to warn a nightshirted Jefferson standing on his front porch in dawn's early light that the British were marching on Monticello to take him prisoner.

Most of today's visitors to that historic mountaintop shrine near Charlottesville dismiss Jouett's hazardous journey as merely a minor incident in the broad panorama of early American history. They will cite the well-publicized midnight gallop of Paul Revere as a more significant historical event. Yet, according to the facts, Jouett's ride through wild Virginia countryside on the night of June 4-5, 1781, makes Revere's Massachusetts jaunt seem trivial by comparison.

Without Henry Wadsworth Longfellow, Revere probably would be remembered today only as a remarkably good silversmith rather than an American Revolutionary War hero. For the truth is, Revere never did all the things that Longfellow gave him credit for in his epic poem, "The Midnight Ride of Paul Revere."

In sallying forth to alert the Massachusetts colonists that the British were coming, Revere covered only 15 of the 30-odd miles between Boston and Concord. To add insult to the situation, he had the humiliation of being captured by the Redcoats! A companion who had joined him during the start of his ride did manage to get through to Concord *two days later* to spread the alarm.

Longfellow, of course, can be excused for exercising an author's prerogative of editorial license in making a hero of Revere with his now-famous lines, "Listen, my children, and you shall hear . . ." It is only natural that patriotic-minded Americans should revere (no pun intended) the memory of all brave colonists who sacrificed so much in the struggle for freedom. Yet had Longfellow been a Southerner, it is quite possible he would have given Captain Jouett hero status, and in this instance with complete justification.

Nevertheless, very little has been recorded of Captain Jouett's hazardous journey in 1781 to warn Jefferson and the Virginia General Assembly meeting in Charlottesville of a British plot to capture them. Cer-

Thomas Jefferson (National Historical Park)

tainly the dangers and hardships he braved when he rode off into the night to sound the alarm at Monticello were far greater than those Revere encountered during his abortive dash from Boston. Yet, sad to state, Jouett's is an important ride that our nation forgot.

Nearly five years had elapsed since America's colonists had begun their fight for independence. Now during the final days of April, 1781, Lord Cornwallis' forces were moving into Virginia from North Carolina. By mid-May the British commander had captured Petersburg, 25 miles south of the Old Dominion capital of Richmond where the Virginia Legislature was in session. With the fall of Petersburg, Richmond faced imminent capture.

Three times since the beginning of that year the assemblymen had fled the city in alarm at reports of Redcoat penetration along Virginia's southern border. On May 20, Governor Thomas Jefferson adjourned the Legislature with plans to reassemble May 24 in Charlottesville, 70 miles west of Richmond in the foothills of the Blue Ridge Mountains.

Jefferson, who had succeeded Henry as Governor in 1779, was approaching the end of his term. His had not been an easy tenure in the Governor's chair. His administration had been hard-pressed by lack of resources, both financial and military. Now the Governor wanted to be sure the Legislature did not adjourn prematurely until his successor had been named, freeing him to return to his beloved Monticello.

It wasn't until May 28 that a quorum of the Legislature convened at Charlottesville. Even then the assemblymen put off selecting a new Governor. So Jefferson's term expired with no one named, forcing him to continue in office.

Early on the morning of June 4, Colonel Banastre Tarleton, a British cavalryman famed as the "hunting leopard," was dispatched with 250 splendidly mounted

THE RIDE A NATION FORGOT

horses to cover the 70 miles between Lord Cornwallis' headquarters, outside Richmond, and Charlottesville. His instructions specifically called for him to seize Jefferson, disperse the Virginia General Assembly, and destroy any of Jefferson's personal property.

Shortly after sundown that day, Tarleton and his troops galloped up the Richmond Turnpike to Cuckoo Tavern, an inn located in Louisa County about 35 miles east of Charlottesville. Here Tarleton ordered a brief halt.

It so happened that Captain Jack Jouett, a member of the Virginia Militia, who was 27 years old, was visiting his family at Cuckoo Tavern when Tarleton and his men arrived. The elder Jouett was owner and proprietor of the inn. Captain Jouett, either by feigning drunkenness or heavy sleep, managed to conceal his identity from the Redcoats while eavesdropping on their conversation. He quickly divined Tarleton's plans from remarks passed among the soldiers and he knew he must act without delay if Jefferson and the legislators were to be saved. He lost no time slipping unnoticed from the inn and quickly set out on horseback for Monticello.

By following seldom used byways and shortcuts, Jouett knew he could avoid the British who were traveling the main turnpike. He also had the advantage of darkness, for the moon was late in rising that night. And he knew the countryside well.

Born in Albemarle County (adjacent to Louisa) on December 7, 1754, Jack Jouett was uncommonly familiar with that part of Virginia. He was also an outstanding horseman. These factors, combined with a robust constitution, favored Jouett during his trying journey.

A man of less stamina might have dropped exhausted from the saddle long before the hectic ride was over. Jouett, however, was a dedicated patriot—he had no thought of abandoning his race with the British until Jefferson had been warned. Mile after tortuous mile he spurred his horse onward.

Dawn was just breaking when Jouett arrived at Jefferson's front door. He guided his horse right up the stone steps and gave a loud call. A sleepy Jefferson came to the portico still in his nightshirt and listened quietly to Jouett's warning of Tarleton's approach. Then the young Captain turned his horse away from the mansion and dashed down the mountainside to Charlottesville where most of the Virginia legislators were staying.

Fully aware of the impending danger, Jefferson began making preparations for his family to leave Monticello for the safety of Blenheim, a neighbor's estate some miles away. Jefferson showed no lack of personal courage. He went about his chores in a calm manner. Then he and one or two members of the Virginia Assembly who were staying with him at Monticello breakfasted "at leisure." Afterwards the Governor spent nearly two hours securing most of his important papers. Finally Jefferson gave orders for his horse to be saddled in readiness for his departure. The legislators who had been visiting the Governor asked for their own horses and rode off to safer havens.

Later Jefferson took up one of his spy glasses and strolled down a wooded path to a nearby clearing where he commanded an excellent view of Charlottesville. Here he saw no signs of the enemy. Perhaps Jouett's warning would turn out to be a false alarm. The Governor took another look, then replaced the glass in its case and started back towards the house. As he did so, Jefferson remembered he had left his valued walking stick leaning against a tree at the edge of the clearing. He turned back and quickly found the stick. Then for some reason he decided to have another look at the village below.

This time Jefferson saw British troops coming up the mountainside toward Monticello. Clouds of dust arose as a detachment of Tarleton's Redcoats galloped up the road. The British were indeed coming!

Jefferson hurried back to his horse tethered nearby. As he leaped into the saddle, he glanced back toward his home. The English soldiers were moving across the crest of the hill onto the spacious lawn. Jefferson hurried off in the direction of Blenheim to join his family.

When he arrived in Charlottesville on the morning of June 5, Colonel Tarleton split his force. Half went up the mountain east of Charlottesville to Monticello. The rest swept through the village itself in search of members of the Assembly. At Jefferson's home the British found two or three servants, but otherwise the house and surrounding buildings were empty.

Tarleton's men took nothing from Monticello other than food and drink. Jefferson is reported to have said afterwards that the British commander "behaved very genteelly with me." The Virginia Governor fared much worse at another of his farms which was visited later by the British troops. He left a record of the pillage. All of his husbanded crops and 150 cattle, sheep, and hogs were seized. All of his growing crops were destroyed. His fences were burned. Not only was his stable of valuable horses stolen, but the throats of colts too young to be used were barbarously slit. Thirty slaves were carried away.

The other half of Tarleton's forces roamed through Charlottesville, tracking down members of the Legislature. A few who failed to heed Jouett's warning were captured. Most of those sought by the Redcoats besides Jefferson—Nelson, Lee, Henry, Harrison—managed to get safely beyond reach of the enemy. Jouett himself eluded capture.

Some time later the Virginia Legislature reconvened in Staunton, 35 miles west of Charlottesville. Here they voted "an elegant sword and pair of pistols" to be presented to Captain Jouett in appreciation of his courage and daring in bringing his timely warning from Cuckoo Tavern to Monticello. The pistols were given to him soon afterwards, but for some unexplained reason the assemblymen neglected to deliver the sword until 1803, long after Jouett had moved to Mercer County (in what is now Kentucky).

A hospitable, attractive, high-spirited man who entertained lavishly and made friends easily (among them Henry Clay, Andrew Jackson, the Breckenridges, and the Marshalls), Jouett later rose to local prominence in Kentucky. He represented Lincoln and Mercer counties in the Virginia Assembly for several terms after the British defeat at Yorktown and before Kentucky was admitted to statehood. Considered an able, aggressive statesman of the Jeffersonian school, Jouett strongly influenced the move to organize Kentucky as a separate state in 1792.

A number of his descendants now live in Kentucky. His son Matthew Harris Jouett, who studied in Boston with Gilbert Stuart, was the first prominent painter in the Middle West. Matthew Jouett's portrait of Lafayette, one of more than 300 paintings he did for friends and on commission, now hangs in the Kentucky capitol building at Frankfort.

A grandson, James Edward Jouett, was one of Admiral Farragut's officers during the War Between the States. The authoritative *Columbia Encyclopedia* lists separately both Jack Jouett's son Matthew and *his* son James, but there is absolutely no mention of the Revolutionary War patriot or his ride.

Jack Jouett died March 1, 1822, while on a trip back to Virginia. Although the exact spot of his grave is unknown, he is probably resting somewhere in the state of his birth—an unsung hero of the Revolution who has all but been forgotten in the 188 years since he made his dramatic ride through the backwoods of old Virginia.

THE SALE OF ALASKA

by M. Belov

Professor of Geography and History, Arctic and Antarctic Scientific Research Institute, Leningrad

*I*t is a widespread opinion in Soviet historical writing that foreign policy considerations—secret czarist diplomatic intrigues to bring Britain and the United States into conflict and, by weakening the British, to regain the Russian positions on the Black Sea that were lost in the Crimean War (1853-1856)—played the main part in the sale of Alaska. But was this really so?

Getting to the bottom of the century-old secret is no easy matter. Researchers still lack documents of paramount importance concerning the strictly confidential negotiations between the Russian court and the American government. An eloquent silence was also maintained by the Russians directly involved in the negotiations.

The circle of authorized persons was so small that

when Alexander II affixed his signature to the main document of the deal on May 3, 1867, only one official was present in his office in the Winter Palace, and that was Prince Gorchakov, Russia's Minister of Foreign Affairs. What the czar said to his minister at the time, as well as the motives which guided him in turning over Alaska to the United States, remain a mystery.

Since public opinion in Russia was opposed to the sale of Russian America, the czarist court, anxious to avoid discussion of the matter, was in no hurry about publishing the actual documents, in particular the Convention on Alaska. The latter was printed only a year later, in French, the diplomatic language of the period, in the "Diplomatic Yearbook" for 1868, a St. Petersburg publication that reached a narrow circle of readers.

While giving no explanation whatsoever to many questions that troubled the public, the Convention gave an exhaustive answer to the main question, which was whether Alaska was being turned over to the United States for good. The answer is contained in the first two articles, the other four fixing the sum to be paid for Alaska and the dates of payment, and also stipulating the right of the Russian settlers to retain their religious beliefs and choose their citizenship.

"His Majesty the Emperor of All Russia," declares Article 1 of the Convention, "undertakes, by this Convention, to concede to the United States, immediately following exchange of the papers of ratification, sovereign rights over all the territory on the American continent now belonging to His Majesty, as well as the adjacent islands; the said territory, situated within the geographical borders indicated below, namely: the eastern border is the demarcation line running between the Russian and British possessions in North America . . the western border of the ceded territory passes through a point in the Bering Strait formed by the intersection of the parallel 65 degrees 35 minutes northern latitude with the meridian equidistant between Krusenstern Island ... and Ratmonoff Island. ...

"Regarding the territory ceded under the previous Article to United States sovereignty, there is granted the right of possession of all lands, common places, free areas, all public structures, forts, barracks, and other buildings that are not private property." (Article II.) The Convention did not deal with the leasing of Alaska but with its sale to the United States forever.

Alaska was discovered by the Russians after Siberia and the Far Eastern regions, in the forties of the 18th century, although the first expeditions in that direction were undertaken a century earlier. In 1648, Semyon Dezhnev, a Cossack from Yakutsk, and his companions, sailing in boats they had made themselves, were the first to sail down the strait dividing the Asian and American continents. In 1732 a Russian expedition led by Ivan Fyodorov and Mikhail Gvozkyov approached the northeastern coast of Alaska.

The actual discovery of America from the East took place later, in 1741, when Vitus Bering and Alexei Chirikov, sailing from Kamchatka in the packet boats *St. Peter* and *St. Paul* respectively, reached the American coast. The Russian seamen made their first landing on Kayak Island, where they saw "great lights and the tracks of man and foxes." This was followed by other important discoveries, including the mouth of the Mednaya River, the rocky Kodiak Island, and the Ukamok, Shumaginskiye and Andreanovskiye islands.

The news about America excited Siberia's traders. So many of them were eager to buy up beaver and sealskins that, according to official figures, 42 Russian expeditions visited the American lands between 1745 and 1764. The discovery and development of the Aleutian chain and other islands in the North Pacific are associated with the names of Savva Ponomaryov, Pyotr

Shishkin, Ivan Solovyov, Stepan Glotov, Vasily Shilo and many other traders.

The first two or three decades of voyages to America were highly reminiscent of the colorful development of Siberia in the 16th and 17th centuries, when thousands of army men, merchants and traders crossed the Urals and, moving "to meet the sun," opened up new lands rich in fur-bearing animals, built palisaded forts and winter quarters, founded towns, started mining ore and salt, and farmed the land.

This was large-scale peasant colonization under the supervision of a feudal state. An important point was that serfs who escaped to Siberia were not returned to their masters. This policy bore fruit. A hundred years after the famous campaign of Yermak (1581) who, as Marx put it, laid "the beginning of Asian Russia," Siberia was a Russian territory in population and main economic setup.

A different destiny lay in store for Alaska. Despite the frequent expeditions not a single permanent Russian settlement appeared there in the first 30 years after the voyage of Bering and Chirikov. In 1784, a merchant named Grigory Shelekhov founded the first residence on Kodiak Island. Eighteen years later, in 1802, Novo-Arkhangelsk, the first "capital," was established on Sithka Island.

Why the delay? Why was the rapid penetration of the Russians into America not accompanied by similarly rapid settlement, as in Siberia?

We must reject at once the supposition that Alaska's remoteness could be the cause, although it did play no small part. The distance from Irkutsk to the Russian trading posts in Alaska was about the same as from Irkutsk to Moscow. Traveling such a distance was, of course, a difficult task. However, the settling of Siberia shows that big distances were never a hindrance to Russian travelers and navigators. Along forest trails and across the Arctic seas these courageous men established uninterrupted connections with the most remote parts of Siberia.

The harshness of the Alaskan climate is sometimes cited as an explanation, but the Russian Columbuses had their own opinion on that score. "The winter there is quite short, with little snow . . . there is sufficient land suitable for settlement," wrote Grigory Shelekhov.

The answer must be sought not in geographical factors but in changes that took place in the 18th century and the first half of the 19th century in the domestic policy of the Russian feudal state, which had entered a stage of crisis. Migration to the eastern regions of the empire, including Alaska, was greatly influenced by the serf laws of the 1760's that turned the peasants into slaves deprived of all rights.

Later the nobility were given exceptional privileges over the peasants. And it was at this time, as statistics show, that migration to Siberia and the Far Eastern regions dropped sharply. The czarist court pursued with utmost consistency this policy of clamping down on large-scale eastward migration.

Under these circumstances an unenviable destiny awaited every request by Siberian merchants for permission to acquire serfs for transportation to new lands. A typical case occurred in 1790 when Grigory Shelekhov submitted a petition of that kind to Catherine II, stating that his company "needed its own serfs." But the empress firmly refused.

When recruiting people for Alaska the merchants and traders usually had to take declassed elements and even criminals. It is not surprising that there were only a few score permanent Russian settlers in America at the end of the 18th century.

This feudal policy was still in force in 1799, when, after the death of Grigory Shelekhov, who had advocated the amalgamation of the trading companies, the czarist court set up a government monopoly organization named the Russian-American Company to protect and expand the Russian possessions in Alaska.

The company's statute contained a special provision on this matter. "In consideration of the remoteness of the places whither they (the merchants—Author) are bound," it said, "the guberniya authorities are instructed to issue passports valid for a period of seven years to government settlers and other free men (at the end of that period these persons returned—Author); as for peasants and manor serfs of landlords (the majority of Russia's peasants—Author), they are to be hired by the company only with the consent of their landlords...."

In other words, the Russian-American Company was told to go begging to the landlords, who as a rule turned down their requests. When the Russian-American Company asked the State Council to release serf peasants the council categorically refused to, and, in a decision passed in 1808, pointed out that the release of peasants without the consent of their landlords would be an infringement of the interest of the nobility.

Many Russians of moderate views, not to mention the Decembrists who put forward a sweeping program of development of the productive forces of Alaska and the Far Eastern regions, repeatedly drew the czar's attention to the need to settle Alaska, regarding that as a sure means of its retention by Russia. In 1803, for instance, State Chancellor N. P. Rumyantsev presented a project to set up populous Russian settlements in Alaska, promote industry and commerce there, build factories operating on local raw materials, and establish towns.

In 1806, an analogous proposal on ways and means of building up the company was made by N. P. Rezanov, its virtual chief, who wrote: "Since the true vigor of those regions should consist of a large number of settlements and inhabitants, more Russians must be invited

THE SALE OF ALASKA

to go there. . . ." He justifiably reproached the government for not following "the far-sighted concepts of Peter the Great" in this respect.

For one reason or another, however, none of these proposals was followed up. The result was that, according to the estimates of scholars, in 1817 there were about 600 Russians on the vast territory of the 5,000 kilometer strip of Alaska. Nor did the situation improve as time passed. In 1866, just before the sale of Alaska, the entire non-indigenous population, including Americans, numbered 800.

One cannot help marveling at the large amount of development and study of Northwestern America carried out by the company with such meager manpower resources (this is not meant to gloss over or justify its brutality towards the backward local population). The company initiated grain and vegetable farming and the opening of schools and libraries. It encouraged scientific expeditions and voyages (Zagoskin's expedition to the Yukon, Khromchenko's expedition to the Bering Strait).

The region's mineral wealth was studied. The credit for the discovery of gold there goes to the Russians. There were attempts to set up a metallurgical industry. The company mapped the coast of Northwest America and published atlases (Tebelkov's and others). The period during which the company functioned left a deep imprint on the history of that distant region of America.

None of that was important enough, however, as the absence of large-scale colonization could not but weaken the company and the Russian positions in Alaska as a whole, and in the long run this led to its loss.

Another question arises. Did Russia attempt to hold onto Alaska with the help of its military force? Yes, such an attempt was made. From the beginning of the 19th century forts with small garrisons were set up

New Archangel, the principal town of Russian Alaska.
(Culver)

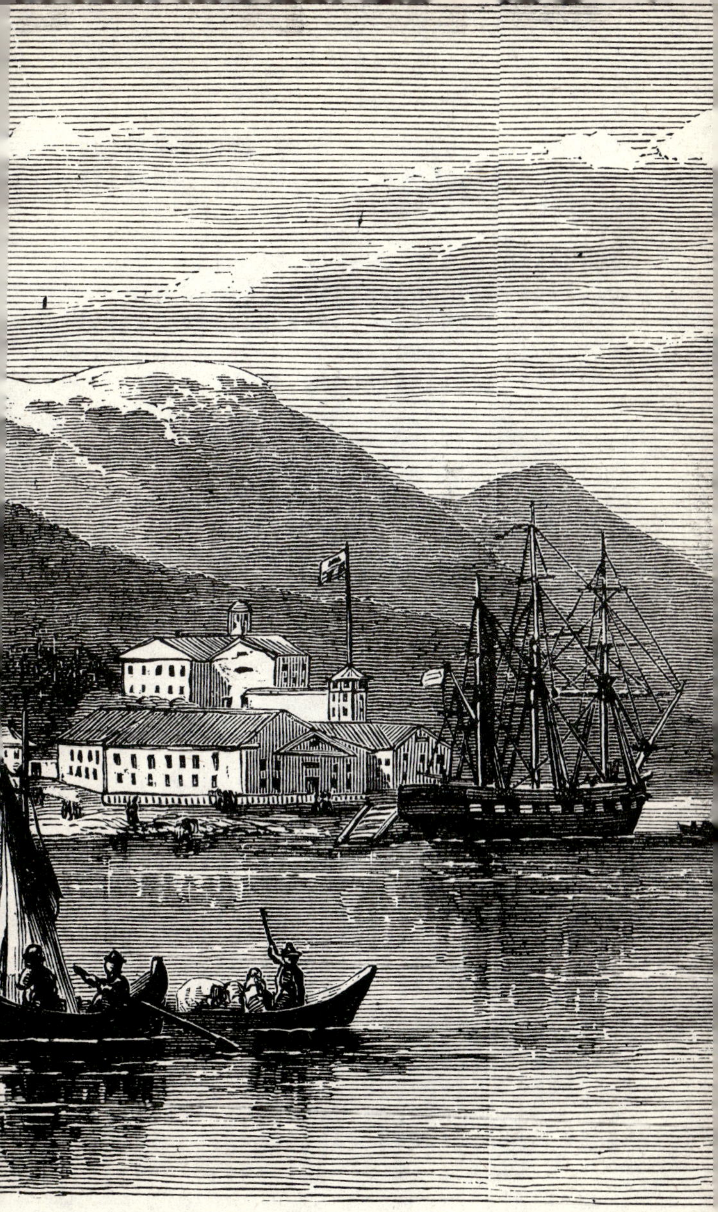

along the coast and on islands of Northwest America. True, there were few of them, and they did not turn out to be strong enough.

During the course of half a century the czarist government outfitted warships to the Pacific Ocean, on what were called round-the-world and halfway-round-the-world expeditions, to support the forts, supply the forts, supply them with provisions and military equipment, and also to demonstrate its navy. The expeditions were headed by Krusenstern, Lisyansky, Golovin, Vasilyev, Wrangel and other outstanding navigators of the period, whose geographical discoveries and important studies of the world ocean brought glory to the Russian navy.

However, the dispatch of warships and the forces of the small garrisons in an environment where people were incited by crafty American and British businessmen could not achieve the desired results. Realizing the weakness of the Russian-American Company, the American and British businessmen began building up forces, while the czarist government's entire inept policy merely aggravated the situation.

For example, in the 1820's Shelekhov's followers, that is, Russian merchants, were ousted from the company management and replaced by czarist ministry officials who looked on the company primarily as a source of personal enrichment. Before long the czarist court curtailed the company's original privileges which had given it a powerful and virtually monopoly position.

Conventions concluded in 1824 and 1825 gave British and United States ships access to all Alaskan inland waters for the purpose of fishing and trading with the native population. This entailed considerable losses to Russian industry and commerce there.

As a concession to Britain, a so-called ally in the Near East, a contract was signed in 1839, with the

THE SALE OF ALASKA

czar's permission, regulating relations between the British Hudson Bay Company and the Russian-American Company. Under this contract part of the Russian possessions on the northwestern coast of America was leased to the British. The contract is rightly regarded as the first step in the cession of the Russian colonies in Alaska.

Not feeling itself to be sufficiently secure in Alaska and the Pacific, the czarist court yielded more and more to foreign pressure, particularly after the defeat in the Crimean War. It was then that the question arose: Could Russia retain its American colonies if they were attacked by a naval power, by Britain or the United States?

When this straight question was put by Finance Minister Knyazhevich, Grand Duke Konstantin, chief of the Russian naval staff, gave an unequivocal reply: "In the event of a war with a naval power," he wrote, "we would not be able to protect our colonies."

Meanwhile, offers for the purchase of Alaska were being made to the czarist court. We cannot agree with those who maintain that the initiative in this matter came from the Russian government. The following should be clearly understood: Regardless of how Russia had been weakened by the Crimean War, regardless of the czarist court's past mistakes in relation to Alaska, and regardless of how weak the Russian-American Company was, none of these factors, either separately or together, would have been the first to raise the question of the transfer of the Russian territories in America to the possession of another power.

Despite it all, Alaska would have remained a possession of the Russians, of those who had discovered and developed it. As an example we can point to our Far Eastern regions, the Okhotsk territory, Kamchatka and Chukotka, where the czar's authority was nominal rather than actual, and where the state of affairs was far from brilliant and largely reminiscent of that in Alaska.

The initiative in the sale of Alaska—and this, by the way, is understandable—came entirely from the United States. The decisive factors were U.S. expansion and U.S. pressure on czarist Russia, which had been weakened by the Crimean War and which had itself, by the whole of its incorrect attitude to the Russian territories in America, undermined its positions there.

The United States forced czarist Russia to agree to the sale, and it was the United States that stipulated the terms. In the 1860's Russia did not have that great strength. Facing America stood a weakened, corrupt czarist regime that was incapable of defending territory.

A question that is sometimes examined in history writings is this: Why did czarist Russia prefer the United States to Britain, whose expansion in the direction of the Russian possessions in America was also well known? Young, dynamic, expansionist American capitalism had smelled big business and had turned out to be craftier, more aggressive and stronger than British capitalism, old and experienced but weaker in that part of the world.

The list of instances of overt and covert American and British territorial and commercial expansion is a long and varied one: the incitement of local inhabitants, Aleuts and Thlinkits, to rise up against the Russian authorities; the supply of these tribes with arms, including artillery; the solicitation of more and more trading, hunting and other privileges in Alaska; the outright seizure of Russian lands; blackmail; invasion of the forbidden zone, the institution of lawsuits against the company; bribery and, finally, direct threats.

Decembrist Dmitry Zavalishin, who visited Alaska and saw what the American hunting and trading companies were doing there, held that the United States was waging a secret war against Russia in that region. An American told him out and out that they would not rest content until they had made the northern part of the Pacific Ocean their own sea exclusively.

He wrote: "Another example of the crass ignorance of the author of the pamphlet! (a pamphlet by Lilienfeld—Author). As he sees it, the cession of the Russian part of North America was nothing more than a diplomatic ruse by the Russian government which, incidentally, was in exceptional need of ready cash. But the main thing was this: the American Congress recently published the documents on that deal.

"They include, among other things, a report by the American charge d'affaires in which he frankly writes to Washington: from the *economic aspect* this acquisition is not worth a cent so far, but—but thanks to this the Yankees will cut off Britain from the sea on one side and they'll speed up the incorporation of the whole of British North America in the United States. That is the crux of the matter!"

The initial negotiations about the sale of Alaska began in the early fifties but their completion was delayed by the Civil War in the United States. Soon after the war the American government exerted still stronger pressure on the czarist court.

America's ruling classes were very well aware of the importance of this step and its consequences. Their views were aptly expressed by the Chairman of the Foreign Relations Committee who, speaking about the appropriation of funds for the purchase of the Russian territories, pointed to their advantage as a key to the Pacific Ocean.

He said that Alaska, together with the islands, would give the United States a foothold in the Pacific Ocean that would assume what he called the "triumph of civilization." It would be, he said, an American civilization, an American destiny for 600,000,000 people.

THE SALE OF ALASKA

The czarist government, feeling itself incapable of defending its Alaskan possessions in the event of a military conflict, and faced with the alternative of aggravating relations with the United States to the point of war, made a deal with the American government, in secrecy from the Russian-American Company.

ALASKA: FROM RUSSIA WITH LOVE

by David Lindsey

*Professor of History,
California State College, Los Angeles*

The story of Alaska is one of apparent contrast and endless paradox. It is the largest state in the Union, with the smallest population, yet more private airplanes are owned and flown in Alaska per capita than anywhere else in the world. The romance of the gold rush days at the turn of the century has become legend from the widely read books by Jack London, yet few Americans know that the Yukon River is one of the greatest drainage systems in the world, rambling more than 2000 miles and bisecting Continental Alaska from east to west.

Tales of mineral wealth, monumental forest lands, and omnipresent icecaps and glaciers rising out of the fog, and the fabled "passage over the pole" are what most remember from school days—and that the United States bought Alaska from Imperial Russia in a coup engineered by the then Secretary of State. Yet the tenor of those times was similar to widespread differences in public opinion today. The Alaska purchase was as controversial then as the Vietnamese war is now.

A hundred years ago, relations between Russia and the United States long had been traditionally friendly. Similiarities of the two countries are readily apparent. Both occupied immense, rich land areas; both were vigorous and expanding nations; both viewed England as a common hindrance thwarting legitimate ambitions of their own.

Both were seeking to fuse diverse peoples into one nationality and both had battled recent insurrections (Poles in Russia and Confederates in the United States). And both had almost simultaneously released oppressed subjects—the serfs in Russia and the slaves in this country. Oliver Wendell Holmes voiced a shared sentiment in his "America to Russia" poem:

> Though watery deserts hold apart
> The worlds of East and West,
> Still beats the selfsame human heart
> In each proud nation's breast.

During the Civil War while England and France sympathized with the Confederacy, two Russian naval fleets visited New York and San Francisco. Americans saw the visits as gestures of friendship, visible evidence that Russia sided with the Union against possible British and French interference on the South's behalf.

The officers and crews of the ships received a red carpet welcome. The tsar was toasted at public banquets and Secretary of the Navy Gideon Welles' joyous "God bless the Russians!" echoed a grateful nation's feelings. In the general melee of celebration it was forgotten that the Russian fleets may have fled to neutral

American waters to avoid possible bottling-up in home ports should war with Britain erupt.

Under Queen Victoria's reign beginning in 1837, Great Britain's aegis was rising around the world, and her growing domination of the seas worked against the tsar's interests, particularly in the Pacific Northwest where the British grew stronger and the Russians weaker. Grand Duke Constantine, brother of Tsar Alexander II, pressed to offer Alaska to America even after a fictitious sale to a San Francisco based commercial company failed to materialize. Russians in Alaska were squeezed by necessity to attempt negotiations with other interests.

During the Crimean War with England in the mid 1850's the English Hudson's Bay Company in Canada and the Russian-American Company, a quasi-governmental corporation which had administered Alaska since 1799, had made a separate agreement removing their respective holdings from the theater of hostilities. However, without adequate aid from Mother Russia, Alaskan endeavors were in bad straits financially, and the tsar and his advisors reasoned rightly that in case of another war Alaska would be impossible for them to defend.

In contrast to its volatile relationship with England, Russia had earlier graciously retracted her trading operations to the area north of 54° 40′ to American insistence generated from both California and Puget Sound interests. In 1860, the Minister of Russia at Washington, Baron Edward de Stoeckl, had approached Senator Gwin of California with a roundabout suggestion that the United States buy Alaska outright from Russia.

In a conversation with President James Buchanan, Gwin was authorized to return Stoeckl's query with a firm offer of $5,000,000, which he did. Gwin, like Seward later, nourished dreams of American expansion throughout Alaska and the Pacific. Negotiations floundered, however, when the bitterly fought presidential election and the eruption of civil war convinced Stoeckl to abandon them for more than six years.

In the interim conditions favoring the sale improved. The American-Russian Company's Alaska concession expired in 1862 and was renewed at an annual basis on the tsar's sufferance, and the company's finances deteriorated rapidly. The Russian government faced the unwelcome prospect of being thrust into direct administration of a distant and unprofitable province, indefensible in case of war and subject to increasing American and Canadian poaching along its coast.

After a winter visit to St. Petersburg in 1866-67, Stoeckl returned to America bearing instructions from his foreign office to sell Alaska for no less than $5,000,000 if the United States initiated an offer. Landing in New York on February 15, 1867, he discreetly leaked the news, knowing that mutual friends attorney Robert J. Walker and California Senator Cornelius Cole would pass the word to Seward that Russia was eager to entertain an offer.

William H. Seward had been President Lincoln's Secretary of State and had been wisely retained by Andrew Johnson. A political descendant of John Quincy Adams, an expansionist for territory prohibited to slavery, Seward was an apostle of the Republican idea of Manifest Destiny—a notion rampant in the unified and growing young nation that it was destined to expand to become the leading power in the New World. Then, too, the United States keenly felt the importance of a democratic role in the world at large. In a speech he made during the 1860 campaign at St. Paul, Minnesota, Seward envisioned the peaceful expansion of his nation over the whole of the North American continent and stated the new, central capital would be "not far" from where he stood and spoke.

ALASKA: FROM RUSSIA WITH LOVE

Seward jumped at the chance offered by Stoeckl while entertaining the Russian at his Washington home. The two men, eager to finalize negotiations, roused even the prima donna senator from Massachusetts, Charles Sumner, along with many clerks from the Russian legation and the State Department. At four in the morning of March 30, 1867, both bleary-eyed and weary, Seward and Stoeckl scrawled their signatures on a hastily prepared document which would transfer Russian Alaska to the United States.

Few Americans then knew anything of Alaska, and the public press hooted in derision at the "dark deed done at night" by a "daft" Secretary of State. The "shrewd Russians" had palmed "Walrussia" off on the silly administration of Andrew Jackson—not the most popular president of all time. Alaska was a "land of short rations and long twilights," "a barren, worthless, God-forsaken region." What madness was "Seward's folly" to pay for "walrus-covered iceburgs!" Alaska was "a national icehouse," "Johnson's Polar Bear Garden," "Seward's Icebox!"

A *New York Herald* advertisement jeered: "CASH! CASH! CASH! Cash paid for cast-off territory. Best price given for old colonies, North or South. Any impoverished monarch retiring from the colonization business may find a good purchaser by addressing W. H. Seward, Washington, D.C." Many Americans agreed that Russia had hoodwinked Seward and passed off on them an imperial-sized Alaska in reality quite worthless.

Stoeckl, authorized by his government to sell for $5,000,000, played a shrewd hand. On the second day of negotiating Seward upped the bid to $5,500,000, raised it another million during the third interview insisting he could not wring another penny out of Johnson's cabinet. But the Russian, sensing Seward's bird dog drive, held firm. Finally Seward agreed to $7,000,000, with an added $200,000 to cover exchange

205

An Alaskan fishing village in 1869. (Culver)

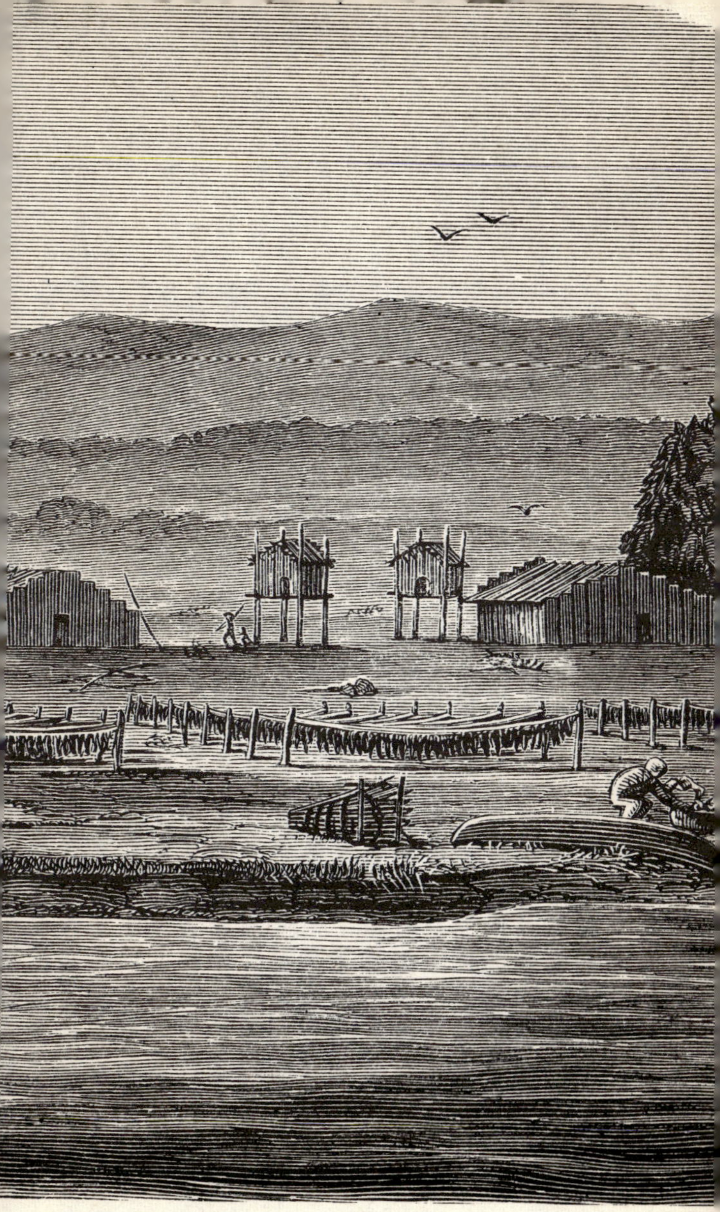

costs and erase existing encumbrances—all this to be paid "in gold at Washington" within ten months after ratification.

In return, Seward incorporated at three points within the treaty that "cession, with the right of immediate possession" of Alaska would be "complete and absolute . . . immediately upon the exchange of ratifications." As events turned out, Seward's insistence upon immediate possession carried the day despite the horrendous difficulties he faced in ramming the Alaska Purchase through Congress. As least from October of 1867 until the gold was transferred to Russia in July of 1868, the United States was in possession of the territory.

About the only issue on which there was no argument in negotiating was that of boundaries. Later, when Canada made claims against the United States, a 1903 tribunal voted in favor of the United States and the original Russian agreement. Seward did lose one or two Aleutian Islands earlier offered, but he managed to settle the difficulties of church lands and citizenship by offering more cash.

Seward had good reason to rush the March 30th predawn treaty signing. Congress was due to adjourn the following day, and within hours Seward was on Capitol Hill pleading his case. But prospects for ratification seemed hopeless as the Senate scheduled a special executive session to run for April's first three weeks. Political antagonisms, totally unconnected to the treaty's merits, militated against Senate approval. These were primarily concerned with the exceedingly unpopular Johnson and the Republican landslide the year before which undermined the administration.

A consummate politician, Seward did not underestimate his opposition. Perceiving his most voluble opponents to be the most ignorant of Alaska's resources, Seward launched a "campaign of education." His press releases underscored the richness of Alaska's fisheries, furs, timber, and minerals and hailed the future thrust of American trade in the Pacific. When Senator Charles Sumner, Foreign Relations Committee Chairman, privately urged Seward to withdraw the treaty, Seward refused and eventually persuaded Sumner to change his own position.

Sumner was the Senate's most polished orator, and his pivotal post gave him power enough to make or break the treaty. After a brief but intense study of Alaska, he blossomed forth into a vigorous campaign of ratification and delivered a compelling, three hour speech on the senate floor. His appeal to commercial interests, Manifest Destiny, democracy, and patriotism (that strange blend of idealism and materialism so often dictating American foreign policy) turned the trick. When the vote came, 27 ayes topped 12 nays (6 absent)—a shift of two votes would have lost the treaty.

It was Sumner who, during this speech, tacked the name of Alaska to what had been formerly known as Russian America. "Alaska" was the Aleut Indian name for "Great Land" and referred originally to the whole of the North American continent, but this corruption was restricted in time to refer to only the southern peninsula of Russian America. Sumner instilled into the name much of the magic and lure of the magnificent scenic area which remains today.

Other hurdles loomed before the American flag would fly over the north country. Ratifications were to be exchanged within three months of the signing on March 30. In late April the Russian Legation's secretary departed for St. Petersburg, secured the tsar's signature, and returned to Washington by mid June. Seward and Stoeckl exchanged formal ratifications on June 20th, a scant ten days before the deadline, and the treaty was officially proclaimed in force.

Opposition in the House of Representatives, which had yet to supply the smaller matter of funds for the

Alaska, 1869. Such pictures became the popular image of the new American possession. (Culver)

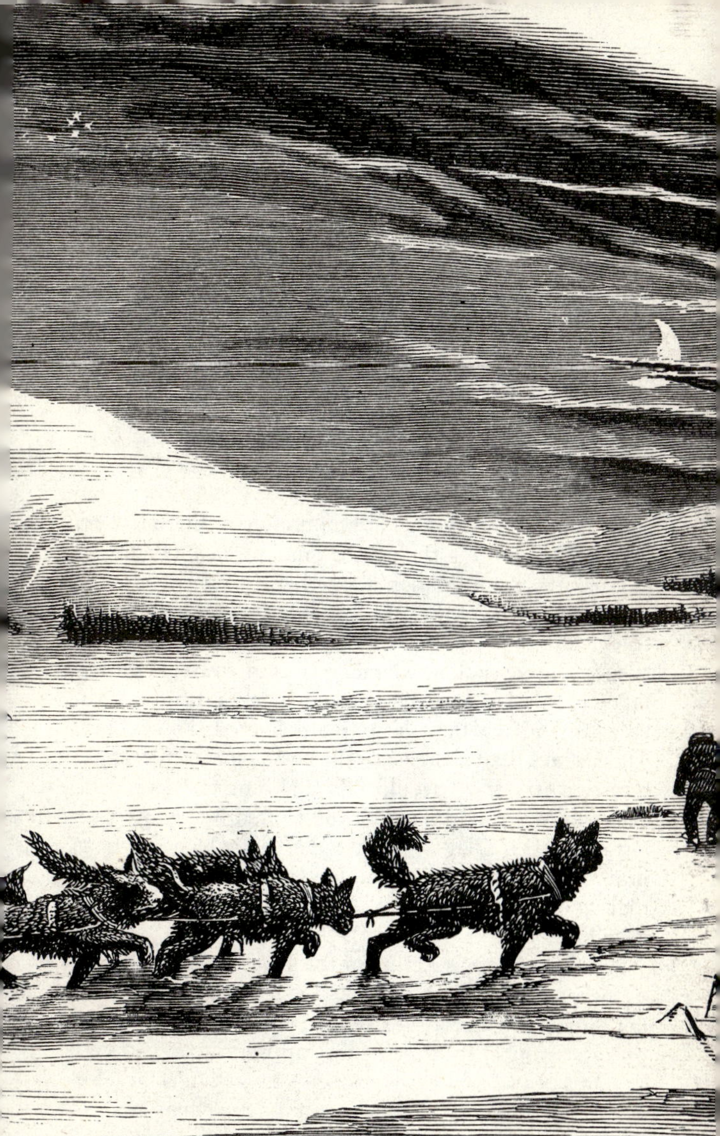

purchase, sprang from diverse sources. Many members were outraged that Seward had committed them to spend $7,200,000 without prior consultation. The *fait accompli* rankled. Others resented Seward's close association with Johnson. "Russia had sold us a sucked orange . . . an icehouse, a worthless desert," they charged, so that Seward could "cover up the mortification . . . he had suffered with the shipwrecked Southern policy of Andrew Johnson."

Two congressmen dug up an old claim of a Benjamin Perkins of Worcester, Massachusetts, against the Russian government for arms ordered during the Crimean War but not delivered before the war's end. They now threatened to delay the appropriation until the claim was settled, or to withhold the amount of $500,000, or to block the appropriation altogether.

Proponents advanced the familiar arguments: Russia's friendship, payment as "an act of recompense to a tried friend," the economic, commercial and strategic importance of Alaska, and the need to block British annexation. An Indiana Representative delivered the clincher: The United States already held possession of Alaska; to refuse to pay for it would be an affront to Russia and, even worse, would humiliate the United States by hauling down Old Glory. "Should the flag which waves so proudly there now be taken down? Palsied be the hand that would dare remove it! Our flag is there, and there it will remain!"

Amid thunderous applause the House passed the appropriation by a vote of 113 to 43. With a puff of relief, Stoeckl, who claimed he had used $165,000 of the purchase price to grease the appropriation through Congress, asked his government to assign him elsewhere to "breathe a purer atmosphere than that of Washington."

The United States barely stood by Seward's original treaty. It was ratified within ten days of the deadline, and the payment was finally appropriated on July 14, 1868, within four days of the ten month deadline after transfer of Alaska took place on October 18, 1867. Without the determination of one man, Seward, the treaty and Alaska might have been lost.

As far as Alaska itself was concerned, the fanfare of arguments and harassment ceased on the afternoon of October 18, 1867. Some two hundred soldiers disembarked from three American naval vessels in Sitka Harbor and filed through the single street of the old Russian town of Baranof Hill and the residence of Prince Dimitri Maksoutoff, the Russian-American Company's manager. Some 60 Russian troops were drawn up close by, while assorted civilians and officials milled about.

At 3:00 p.m., to the boom of military cannon, the double eagled insignia of Imperial Russia was lowered. It caught in the halyard; a marine sent aloft unfastened it and hurled it down on the heads of the Russian soldiers. Young and lovely Princess Maksoutoff, wife of the company manager, brushed back tears as the Stars and Stripes rose up the flagpole to symbolize passing of Alaska from the rule of her motherland.

The Russian Commissioner, Captain Alexei Petchouroff, spoke a few words of transfer. General Lovell H. Rousseau, American Commissioner, signified his acceptance. "The Russian eagle has now given place to the American," recorded an *Alta California* reporter. "Our dominion now borders a new ocean and almost touches an old continent—Asia." The thought that "democratic institutions now extend over an area hitherto possessed of a despotic government . . . inspired the soul of every American present . . . and we all rejoiced that we stood on American ground."

The Alaska territory contains 586,000 square miles, an area larger than Texas, California, New York, New Jersey, and five more New England states combined. Bought at less than two cents apiece, Alaska's 375,000,000 acres were to eventually attract more than a quarter million residents, and in time Russia's "frozen asset" literally became an American gold mine in spite of decades of public and governmental neglect.

Against the $7,200,000 reluctantly paid for Alaska, the revenues returned to the United States during the first forty years of off-handed possession totaled $9,555,909 from rentals, taxes on sealskins, customs collections, sales of public lands, and from other sources. It was estimated that in the same period the United States drew from Alaska fish, furs, and gold to the value of about $150,000,000; that up to 1903 the imports from the States aggregated some $100,000,000; and that $25,000,000 of American capital had been invested in Alaskan ventures, a fair return from a "walrus-covered icebox."

Russians living in Alaska at the time of transfer were given a choice of American citizenship after three years, but the majority preferred to return to their homeland. Because of the unpopularity of the purchase in the United States, control of the territory passed immediately after to the army. In 1877 a serious revolt of native Alaskans caused the white settlers at Sitka to appeal for army aid (withdrawn to fight the Indian wars in the American West), and the British responded at once, sending a frigate to the area by March 1, 1877. Several months later, in June, the *USS Jamestown* arrived at Sitka Harbor, and for the next five years the navy controlled Alaska.

Finally in 1884, through the Organic Act, laws pertaining to the Oregon Territory were extended where applicable to Alaska, and from 1912 until statehood Alaska was governed as a bona fide United States territorial possession. Development of the area was consequently slow; not until the early 1900's was the Homestead Act extended to Alaska to enable settlers to own land, and the government finally in the interests of conservation controlled the taking of fur-bearing animals after the seals and walrus were practically extinct.

Discovery of gold on the Yukon in 1880 and near Nome in 1900 brought an onslaught of population to the region, but when the more easily found mines were exhausted, most returned to the "outside" as the rest of the United States is known in Alaska. During the depression years of the Thirties, however, when the price of gold again rose and Alaska was heralded by many as a new frontier, a new migration began. The beloved Will Rogers was killed when reporting on Alaska in 1935 as he flew north to Point Barrow, the northernmost point on the North American continent.

Following World War II, pressure to admit Alaska to the Union increased. Not only had the strategic location of the state been proved, but many servicemen stationed there returned to settle after the war. Government interest itself had been aroused, and discovery of mineral wealth turned up vast reserves of coal, lead, timber, gold, mercury, platinum, and oil. In the 1960's, export of oil matched in dollars the combined exports of all other industries.

On January 3, 1959, President Eisenhower signed Alaska into statehood, and the new state constitution went into effect. Different from all other state governmental divisions, Alaska has no counties, but restricts its local governments to boroughs, whether settled or not, yet the legislature has never set up any boroughs and the electing units remain an original twenty-four "election districts."

Despite the growing industry and the growing influx of people into Alaska, government remains, as it has been from the first, the biggest power in the state. In 1965, forty-two percent of the employed worked directly for the United States government. The problems and hopes of Alaska's future still rest, as they did in

ALASKA: FROM RUSSIA WITH LOVE

1867 and 1877 and again in 1964, upon the interest of the federal government in Washington, D.C.

Information about the state is best obtained by writing to a state agency, or federal one. Practically all land in Alaska is still publicly owned; there remain limitations on export of lumber, gold mining, fishing, fur catching (only natives are now allowed to take seals and walrus), and practically every other business in the state including retailing, as Alaska is still without continental fair trade shipping rates. Ironically enough, America's new frontier is its most government-controlled area.

The success and enthusiasm in Alaska today are a healthy indication of recovery from the earthquake, one of the most powerful ever recorded, which hit Anchorage and south central Alaska on March 27, 1964. Damage from the quake and subsequent sea wave included 114 lives lost and loss of property estimates ran into three quarters of a billion dollars. President Lyndon Johnson declared Alaska a major disaster area and sent an immediate $5,000,000 from his emergency relief fund; later Congress authorized another fifty millions to aid in rebuilding public facilities, matching a sum voted in bonds by the Alaskan legislature.

1967 is Alaska's Centennial as well as that of Canada (formed July 1, 1867), and throughout the state commemorative celebrations have been planned. Fairbanks, as the stopover for "over the pole flights," has been chosen for the site of "A-67," the Alaskan competition of Expo-67 in Montreal. Over $10,000,000 has been invested in the golden domed playground. This summer gold rush days will be recreated, Alaskan industry described, river boats will ply the routes again, and general merrymaking will draw an expected 300,000 tourists—and hopefully some new homesteaders—to the promising land of "twilight nights" and arctic vistas.

MISCHIANZA THE SECRET HISTORY OF BENEDICT ARNOLD

by Robert Hardy Andrews

*C*omposers of epitaphs on monuments, like historians in their textbook footnotes, are likely to tell too little in their effort not to tell too much. The result sets landmarks along roads out of the past that are unreliable guides for those who seek the truth and nothing but the truth. There was, for example, a memorial tablet at the corner of First Avenue and 46th Street in New York, placed there in 1915 by the Daughters of the American Revolution. Few passersby noticed it and fewer stopped to study it. This may have been because it was set in the wall of a packing company's slaughter-house. In any event the tablet disappeared when the ugly old abattoir was torn down to make way for the shining United Nations citadel. No marker remains, to remind posterity: Near this site Nathan Hale, Captain in the Continental Army, who was apprehended within the British lines while seeking information for Washington, was executed 22 September 1776. His last words were "I only regret that I have but one life to lose for my country."

That Nathan Hale was a 20-year-old Connecticut schoolmaster who loathed violence yet was one of the citizen soldiers who captured an enemy provisions sloop under the guns of a British man-of-war, that he despised the sordidness of espionage yet volunteered to serve as a spy, that he was self-betrayed by the Yale diploma found in a pocket of his disguise as an immigrant from neutral Holland, that though Sunday church-bells clanged while he was hurried to the scaffold his captors refused his request for a Bible and a chaplain to pray with him, even that his grandnephew's wholly fictional *The Man Without a Country* does cruel injustice to another patriot who died as bravely for the American dream: such details flesh bare bones, but still the story is incomplete. Nor will the searcher find a link with Nathan Hale in what is carved on a slab in a shadowed alcove of England's Westminster Abbey, that salutes the memory of Major John André of the Royal Fusiliers.

There is no mention that he, too, was hanged as a spy, on another Sunday morning, October 2, 1780, at Tappan across the Hudson from Manhattan; or that but for precedent set by his own people in 1776, he might have lived to fulfill the promise that made him, at 29, *beau sabreur* of careerists in the British Army sent to crush rebellion in the Colonies. No record exists of his last words; but witnesses testified he went to the scaffold "with as much ease and cheerfulness of countenance as if he had been going to an Assembly Ball." When the hangman hesitated, "he adjusted the rope around his neck and his own handkerchief over his eyes." Like Nathan Hale, to the last "he seem'd to Value Honour more than Life, and met Death with

Benedict Arnold (Culver)

the Courage of a Hero and the Calmness of a Philosopher." Such praise of any other enemy would have been called treason in the times. It was permissible, and popular, in André's case, because it was generally believed he was the victim not of a military court but of the most execrated fallen idol in American history.

Which brings us to two monuments that tell a tale of treachery because what is not there to be seen or read is nonetheless palpably present. One is a tower 155 feet tall, overlooking the Field of Grounded Arms at Saratoga in the Hudson River valley, where Gentleman Johnny Burgoyne and 5,000 of England's best troops surrendered on October 17, 1777. From niches around the tower's base, sculptured likenesses of three rival claimants to immortality earned at Saratoga frown at posterity that has long forgotten them. A fourth niche is empty. Not far off, a marble shaft marks the spot at which the actual victor fell, shot through the leg and lamed for life but only beginning the career that made him unforgettable. Burgoyne, and George Washington and Benjamin Franklin, credited him with turning the tide of the Revolution; but the shaft records only his rank and the dates of two battles in which he fought, at Freeman's Farm and Bemis Heights, September 19 and October 7, 1777.

The space for the hero's name is blank, because he was Benedict Arnold, and nothing he did before the night of September 21, 1780, can expunge or mitigate his damning epitaph as Franklin wrote it. "Judas sold only one man; Arnold, 3 million. Judas got for his one man 30 pieces of silver; Arnold, not a half-penny a head. A miserable bargainer!" Miserable he was, when on his death-bed Arnold begged to be buried in the American uniform he disgraced. But Franklin's figures were wrong. In fact, he sold only two men, himself and John André; and no other traitor we know of was ever better paid in cash and emoluments, for a treasonous plot that failed—and may never have been meant to succeed.

Only Benedict Arnold, and his young wife who had known André well before she married Arnold, knew then, and no one can be certain now, why with eyes wide open he plunged from a patriot's pedestal into the mire of treachery. Much of his history has been a secret for nearly two centuries. It is, however, possible to surmise much that neither monuments nor texts suggest, from what is known of his public life that ended in London on June 14, 1801. It can even be speculated that his course was charted before he was born, at Norwich, Connecticut, on January 14, 1741.

He was his family's fourth Benedict Arnold in America. The first, his great-grandfather, was three times governor of colonial Rhode Island. The third, his father, was a drunken failure. Arnold's pious, protective mother did all she could for his future by binding him out at 14 to her cousins, who were prosperous apothecaries, as an apprentice-drudge. Rebelling against their discipline, at 17 he ran away to join a company formed in New York to privateer against the French. Soon posted as a deserter, he evaded arrest by losing himself among traders with the Indians north of Albany. At 19, when his parents died, he reappeared in Norwich, remaining only long enough to auction off their homestead, his sole inheritance. With what this brought, he set up shop in New Haven, selling medicines and books, styling himself Dr. Arnold.

Small-framed but tall in assurance, single-minded in pursuit of the main chance, his way of cutting corners and promising more than he paid caused leading citizens to shy off from him. Still he was able to borrow capital and invest in cargoes for the West Indies. Undoubtedly the profits came from smuggling; but few New England fortune-builders in those times were in a position to call kettles black. Their Sunday piety was separate from their week-day round: rum to Africa in exchange for slaves, slaves to the Caribbean in exchange for sugar and molasses, sugar and molasses back to New England to be distilled into rum. If faint praise matters, it should be noted that Arnold was never a slaver.

He bought mules, cattle and horses cheap in Montreal and Quebec and sold them dear at Salem quayside, and bartered with Indians, pinchbeck and brummagem for prime furs. The Indians called him Dark Eagle, not only because he had a predator's profile. White men as well sensed a darkling spirit behind his always searching eyes; but his steady climb gained grudging respect, if not respectability. In 1767, by now possessed of a handsome house in Water Street, he married the catch of the county, Margaret Mansfield, the High Sheriff's daughter, who in five years gave him three sons. He named none Benedict.

He was away on a West Indies venture when news reached him, weeks late, of the Boston Massacre on May 5, 1770. Until then, he had dismissed talks against the British as radicalism bad for business. Shooting was a different matter. "Good God," he wrote, "are the Americans all asleep, and tamely yielding up their liberties, or are they all turned philosophers, that they do not take immediate vengeance?" Back in New Haven, where Nathan Hale would get his Yale diploma three years later, Arnold joined the local militia and at once displayed a talent for command. Elected Captain in December, 1774, he was ready for the business he was born for when on April 19, 1775, at Lexington across the line in Massachusetts, some unknown farmer fired the shot that was heard 'round the world.

Parading his company, he called on New Haven's selectmen to issue ammunition. They hesitated. To ease their fears, he signed a declaration disclaiming "every thought of rebellion to his Majesty as supreme Head of the British Empire, or opposition to legal Authority." Then he led out down the road to Cambridge, ordering his citizen soldiers to load their muskets while he marched them at a dog-trot. In Cambridge, he interrupted deliberations of the Massachusetts Committee for Safety to present a plan for surprise attack on Fort Ticonderoga, aimed both to block a British advance from the north and to capture cannon for use against the British in the siege of Boston. He spoke so compellingly that on May 3 he was commissioned Colonel and authorized to enlist 400 volunteers in western Massachusetts and lead them against Ticonderoga in New York.

His instructions were signed by Dr. Benjamin Church, the committee's chairman, a Boston physician and writer and friend of John Hancock and John Adams, soon after appointed director of hospitals for Washington's Continental Army. Arnold cannot have suspected that for the first time, he saw the false-face of treason; but six months later, under Washington's cross-examination, a woman revealed that to buy gauds for her, Dr. Church had begun selling secret information to the British six weeks before Lexington. Wailing Adam's cry that feminine wiles were his downfall, concurrently claiming he betrayed his countrymen for their own good, hoping to force them out of an immoral war they could not win, Church was jailed at Norwich, Arnold's birthplace.

In 1777, he was kicked out of the Colonies, disowned by both Americans and British. The ship on which he sailed was never seen again, nor was Dr. Church. By then, the Revolution had produced, to set against the first American traitor, two archetypes of impregnable patriotic loyalty: Nathan Hale and Benedict Arnold, to whom Washington wrote from Valley Forge that "A gentleman in France having obligingly sent me three sets of epaulettes and sword-knots, two to be disposed of to any friends I choose, I take the liberty of presenting them to you and General Benjamin Lincoln, as a testimony of my sincere regard and approbation of your conduct." But in 1775, another candidate for glory halted Arnold's rise to fame so summarily, by capitalizing on a single bloodless exploit and a sentence that may or may not have been uttered, that anyone but Arnold might have ridden dudgeon's high horse out of the war.

Seeking recruits at Stockbridge, Massachusetts, Arnold learned that Ethan Allen was already assembling a Ticonderoga expedition at Castleton, Vermont, and rode there at a gallop to show his six-day-old Massachusetts commission. Allen showed his, from the Connecticut Assembly. It pre-dated Arnold's. More importantly, Allen's Green Mountain Boys comprised the bulk of the expeditionary force. The Vermont paladin said no one but he would command, and his Boys supported him. For once, if not often afterward, Arnold accepted second place. Getting to the war mattered more than how he got there; once in action, he would gamble on the outcome. At Lake Champlain, he made sure he was in one of the few boats that could be found to carry eighty-four other raiders across to Ticonderoga on the western shore. There at dawn on May 10, 1775, Allen made a speech, then led up a cow-path, wounded a startled sentry slightly with his sword, waked the sleeping British commandant, and if legend can be trusted, demanded surrender "In the name of the great Jehovah and the Continental Congress!" Oddly, he failed to include this in his flamboyant report; and much else went unreported except by Arnold.

According to him, Allen again refused to grant him any share in command, "because I had forbid the soldiers plundering and destroying private property." Their quarrel went so far that "I awoke to find Allen brandishing his sword and his men aiming their guns at me." Peace was patched together sufficiently for Arnold to find a fight of his own. Recruiting a hundred men under his Massachusetts commission, he seized a British Loyalist's schooner on the lake, sailed it to St. John's beyond the Canadian border, and captured a small British garrison, an armed sloop and some canoes, and a large supply of military stores. This independent adventure made him commander on water if not on land. On May 29, Allen stepped down and went home to receive his imperishable crown. Briefly, then, Arnold held the sole command that was meat and drink to ease his consuming thirst and hunger. But only briefly.

Jurisdictional dispute erupted, between civilians running segments of the war in New York, Connecticut and Massachusetts. The committee headed by Dr. Church sent peremptory orders to Arnold to hand over Ticonderoga to an officer from Connecticut, and return forthwith to face inquiry into allegations of irregularities in his accounts and use of his official position for private profit. To Arnold, this was "a most disgraceful reflection" on him and on his troops, an insult to "my rectitude and abilities," and "sufficient inducement for me to decline serving longer rather than be sacrificed for political reasons." Nor did his way of reacting endear him to his brother officers.

At Crown Point, a new-made Colonel spoke harshly to him. "I took the liberty of breaking his head, and on his refusal to draw like a gentleman, he having his sword at his side and case of loaded Pistols in his pocket, I kicked him very heartily, and ordered him from the Point immediately." This incident was taken as confirmation of the British description of him: "a low fellow, a mere Horse Jockey." Yet subsequently, an English Lord described him as "more like a Gentleman (whatever he may have been) than nine out of ten of the Rebel Generals." Ethan Allen joined the chorus against

Arnold persuading Andre to conceal the papers in his boot.
(Culver)

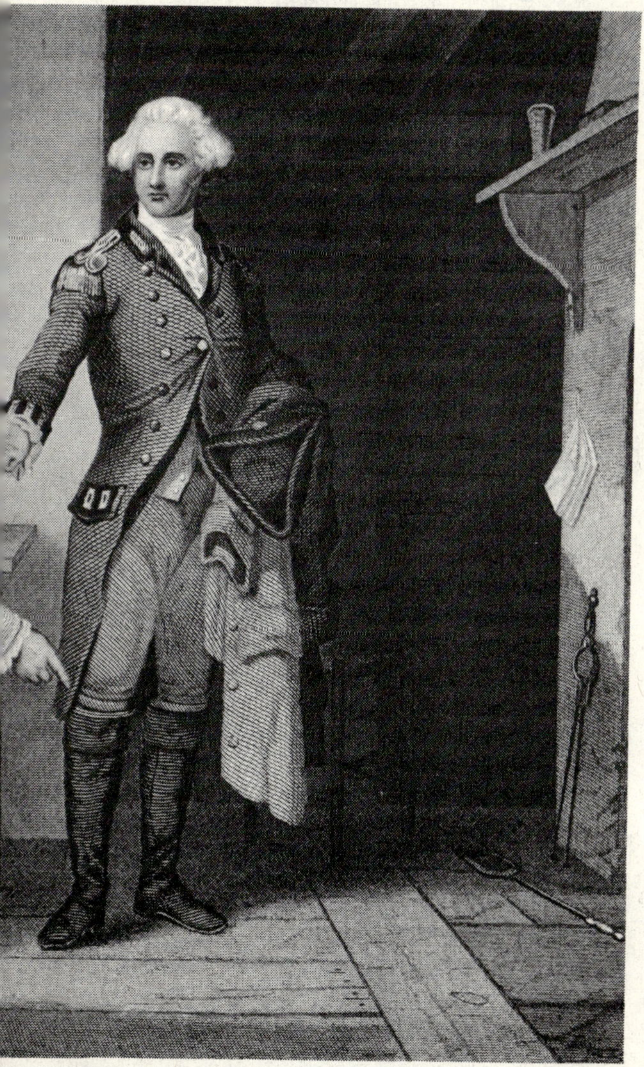

him, when inquiry into his finances was postponed because invasion of Canada was in the making. Allen, he proclaimed, would lay his life on a guarantee that "With fifteen hundred men, and a proper train of artillery, I will take Montreal." Arnold responded. With two thousand men, he said, I will take all of Canada, "but I would want no Green Mountain Boys on the expedition." This earned him more enemies.

In September, 1775, the Continental Congress, now asserting primacy over the colonial committees, made George Washington commander-in-chief of the Continental Army, to be paid $500 per month in salary and expense allowances, and commissioned the first four American Major Generals: wealthy Philip Schuyler, mercenary Charles Lee, doughty old Israel Putnam, and Artemas Ward, erstwhile a sedentary church-warden, by then commanding the siege of Boston. The siege was hurting the British, largely because the rebels now had cannon captured at Ticonderoga. Anonymous among volunteers serving the guns was a newly-commissioned Lieutenant, Nathan Hale. Chosen to command the Canadian thrust was a former British officer, Richard Montgomery. But without consulting Congress, Washington ordered Arnold to lead his own attack on the prime target, Quebec.

Volunteers rushed to join Arnold. Among them was a young glory-hunter from Princeton, Aaron Burr. In 1807, Burr would be charged with treason, and acquitted only on legal technicalities. In 1775, he rose from a sick-bed to ride pellmell after Arnold, already on the march. "The invasion of Canada was a record of heroism, desperate adventure, and glory colored over by weakness and human frailty" capsules a campaign that might have, had it succeeded, created a United States "extending in an unbroken mass from the Rio Grande to the Arctic Ocean"; so at least one scholar summarizes. Ethan Allen reached center-stage well ahead of Arnold, only to be taken prisoner with 40 of his Green Mountain Boys. His British captor growled that he would "grace a halter at Tyburn, God damn ye"; but Allen, shipped to England in chains, was protected by his self-made reputation, and spent the next three years as an imprisoned celebrity.

Montreal fell to Montgomery. En route, at Fort St. Johns, 500 British regulars and volunteers surrendered as prisoners of war. Among them was John André, then a junior Lieutenant. At this time, nothing promised that one day, André and Arnold would meet. Arnold and his miserable and mutinous 700 men, who "more resembled a long file of straggling skeletons than an army of the living," were lost in the wintry woods in Maine. None in his command were harder to keep in line than Colonel Daniel Morgan, whose likeness is one of the three that survey the Saratoga battlefield. But Arnold pressed on, until on November 8, 1775, he was first to stand on the bank of the St. Lawrence looking across at Quebec. At night on November 13, he led a crossing in canoes and dugouts, landing where Wolfe landed in 1759 and launched the attack that completed British conquest of North America. Now Arnold led up to the Plains of Abraham; but the British refused to come out and fight as Montcalm and the French had done when Wolfe was the attacker.

Montgomery arrived, with 300 men and supplies of food and clothing. They agreed that on the first snowy night, they would assault from two sides; and that to minimize desertions under fire, they would lead in person. Neither knew that deserters had betrayed their battle plan. On December 20, rockets gave the signal. Church-bells chimed answer from Quebec. Pointblank cannon fire cut down and killed Montgomery. Aaron Burr tried to hold Montgomery's men together, but panic sent them running away. Arnold, with only 30 followers, ran headlong into a narrow street. Suddenly, a bullet shattered his leg-bone. He fell, lurched up, stumbled on, fell again; and Colonel Morgan took command, but stopped his charge only a little farther on. Had the Americans driven ahead, as they most assuredly would have if Arnold had been there, they might have taken the entire lower town. The opportunity soon passed, however. Morgan, deserted by his men, handed his sword to a priest. "Not a scoundrel of those cowards shall take it out of my hand." The battle for Quebec was lost.

But Arnold would not say die. From his hospital bed, he managed to keep his few hundred hungry, freezing volunteers at their posts, holding Quebec under siege in hope that reinforcements would arrive and attack could be renewed. On April 1, 1776, his hope seemed realized. Arnold mounted to review them, but was thrown from his horse. The fall reopened his wound. Still he insisted on riding to Montreal, where he commanded while at Quebec, a citizen General was out-maneuvered by professionals: Carleton, the British commandant, and Burgoyne. On June 13, Arnold closed this chapter in his history, by writing "The junction of the Canadas with the Colonies is now at an End let us quit them & Secure our own Country before it is too late." This left many ifs for posterity to ponder.

"If Arnold had reached the St. Lawrence a few days earlier, if there had been no short-term enlistments to impel Arnold and Montgomery to attack when they did, if Montgomery had survived and Arnold not been wounded, if Arnold had been given command of the spring reinforcements, these are only a few of the after-thoughts that haunted the military and the politicians in the months that followed. . . It was mainly their deficiencies in organization and training that defeated the Americans. Even so, they came extraordinarily close to winning this most daring and spectacular thrust of the entire war. And no one could ever justly say that they lost for lack of daring and devoted leadership."

No one, that is, but Arnold's critics and sworn enemies. His wife had died while he was away fighting. His complicated financial affairs, left untended, were by now in chaos; he was nearly bankrupt. The last American to leave Canadian soil, on June 17, 1776, he was almost immediately summoned to face charges that at Ticonderoga, he had been too dictatorial in dealing with a Captain who questioned his orders; that in the retreat from Canada, through negligence or for personal gain, he had allowed plunder and waste of stores captured at Quebec; and worst, that when he was superseded at Ticonderoga, he had "planned a treasonable attempt to make his escape . . . to the enemy." Thus "traitor" was cried against him, when all evidence was to the contrary. "I cannot but think it extremely cruel," he wrote while civilians bayed at him from a safe distance, "when I have sacrificed my ease, health, and a great part of my private property in the cause of my country, to be calumniated as a robber and a thief." There was more to come. On March 10, he learned from Washington that the Continental Congress, without consulting him, had promoted five officers, all Arnold's juniors in service "and inferiors in ability," to the rank of Major General. There was no promotion for Arnold.

Washington urged him not to resign. "You are too much needed." He replied: "In justice to my own character and for the satisfaction of my friends, I must request a court of inquiry into my conduct. Though I sensibly feel the ingratitude of my countrymen, every personal injury shall be buried in my zeal for the safety and happiness of my country, in whose cause I have repeatedly fought and bled and am ready at all times to resign my life." Then hearing of Tryon's raid in Connecticut, he rode hard from New Haven to

Ridgefield, assembled 500 militiamen, and fought Tryon's 2,000 British regulars to a standstill. One of his horses was killed, another was wounded. A bullet passed through his coat-collar. Finally, with poor grace, Congress made him a Major General.

Still he was placed in grade below five former Brigadiers who had served under him; and a handbill was circulated posting him as a criminal, with black type proclaiming, "Money is this man's god, and to get enough of it he would sacrifice his country." On July 11, he sent in his resignation. "Honour is a sacrifice no man ought to make; as I received, so I wish to transmit it to posterity." The same day, Congress received a letter from Washington requesting Arnold's assignment to command the northern militia under General Philip Schuyler. "He is active, judicious, and brave, and an officer in whom the militia will repose great confidence." Congress forwarded this to Arnold, who quickly informed Washington that he would withdraw his resignation. "No private or Publick Injury or insult," Arnold wrote, "shall prevail on me to forsake the Cause of my Injur'd & oppressed Country until I see peace & Liberty restored to her, or nobly die in the Attempt." The next day, Congress voted down a resolution to restore his seniority in command "on account of his extraordinary merit," and again censured him for unsatisfactory bookkeeping.

He was already in the field, a volunteer leading volunteers to meet Burgoyne and his grenadiers coming down from Canada. Fort Schuyler lay besieged, and Schuyler's attempt to lift the siege had failed. Arnold wrote: "You will hear of my being victorious, or no more." His officers thought attack was suicidal. Curtly, he told them he preferred "to hazard a battle rather than suffer the garrison to fall a sacrifice." Suddenly, he was the Dark Eagle the Indians knew. Loyalists had recruited them to surround the fort. He played on their superstition, threatening to hang a half-mad Dutch woods-runner they regarded as a witch unless they deserted the British. The ruse worked wonders. The Indians told their Loyalist employers that Dark Eagle was coming with more men than the trees had leaves, then fled. The Loyalists joined the flight. On August 24, the siege ended; and all concerned praised Arnold.

All, that is, but General Horatio Gates, whose likeness is most prominent as a part of the Saratoga Monument. Gates had been Washington's neighbor in Virginia, owed his rank to Washington, but was about to come under a cloud never altogether dispelled, as result of the so-called Conway Cabal, allegedly aimed to put him in Washington's place "at the top of the tottering Liberty Pole." No charge of treasonous intent or act was ever lodged against Gates; but many in the times thought schemers hoped to use him as puppet in negotiating a cease-fire that would have been a British victory. If so, the game was spoiled when Washington sent Arnold to serve under Gates and "prove by further deeds his worthiness of higher rank." Gates labeled him "that pompous little fellow," and placed him with the reserves "to keep him from doing anything rash." But Arnold present where guns fired could not be kept from fighting.

At Freeman's Farm on September 19, ignoring the defensive strategy Gates had decreed, Arnold launched sudden attack on serried British grenadiers, Old Invincibles from European battlefields. Later, Burgoyne told a startled England that when thus well-led, the rebels were a match for the best troops the then-greatest military power on earth could ship overseas to scatter them. But Gates, in his report to Washington, made no mention of Freeman's Farm, or Arnold. On September 22, he quarreled publicly with Arnold, snorting that having once resigned he had no right to command anywhere, and pushing hard to make him leave. But

Arnold stayed, and at Bemis Heights on October 7, rode in among and rallied disorganized volunteers, and again led a headlong charge.

Fighting on his own terms, again using Colonel Daniel Morgan and his riflemen for spearhead as he had at Quebec, he drove to the verge of total victory before his horse was killed under him and a British musket shattered his thigh-bone. Witnesses agreed that if Gates had sent in the reinforcements he asked for, Burgoyne could hardly have postponed surrender, as he did until Saratoga ten days later. Even Gates unbent sufficiently to include "the gallant General Arnold" in his report, noting that Arnold's leg was broken "as he was forcing the enemy's breastworks." If the bullet that lamed him had killed him instead, Arnold's might be the only statue adorning the Saratoga Monument. As it was, while he lay wounded, not only Gates but Morgan and General Lincoln laid claim on the victor's laurels. In England, Edward Gibbon wrote: "I shall scarcely give my consent to further exhaust the finest country in the world in the prosecution of a war from which no reasonable man entertains any hope of success. It is better to be humbled than ruined." In Paris, Benjamin Franklin used the news of Saratoga to push France into alliance that started a flow of money, munitions, men and ships without which final triumph might not have been won at Yorktown, four years to the day after Burgoyne's surrender. But in New Haven, although some soldiers and civilians turned out to cheer and cannon boomed a thirteen-gun salute, Arnold lay reading complaints from Congress committees and tirades published by his enemies.

Warned by Alexander Hamilton that Philadelphia could not be defended, Congress fled to New York, leaving Washington with dictatorial powers he had no means to exercise. Heavy losses at Brandywine on September 11, the "Paoli Massacre" on September 21, decimated the Continental Army. On October 4, Washington struck back desperately at Germantown. That night he reported to Congress: "In the midst of the most promising appearances, when everything gave the most flattering hopes of Victory, the troops began suddenly to retreat; and entirely left the Field, in spite of every effort that could be made to rally them." It cannot have pleased uniformed rivals of "that pompous little fellow," or their friends, his foes in Congress, that hard on the heels of disaster in Pennsylvania came news of Arnold's achievements in New York.

Envy, jealousy, prudence, plain save-himself-who-can, spread from New England to the Carolinas. Independence Day orations to the contrary, the hard pure flame of sacrificial patriotism did not burn bright in every heart during the winter that tried men's souls. At Valley Forge, summer soldiers deserted and the Continental Army starved to a skeleton, while in Philadelphia only twenty-five miles away Sir William Howe and the occupying British were warm, well-fed, gaily confident that finishing their business with the rebels could wait until the weather improved, and feted not only by avowed Loyalists but by erstwhile revolutionists who had turned their coats with the changing of the wind.

Virginia farmers sent their grain to Philadelphia, not to Valley Forge; the British paid in cash, the Continental Army in shin-plasters. When Connecticut imposed a price-ceiling on beef, growers shot their cattle rather than sell them. The Army's civilian contractors let pork for Valley Forge rot in New Jersey while they hauled flour and iron north to the British in New York. At Christmas, Washington told Congress he had "no less than 2898 Men now in Camp unfit for Duty because they are bare foot and otherwise naked." The Marquis de Lafayette, who had joined Washington in time to be wounded at Brandywine, wrote to France:

The capture of Major Andre. (Culver)

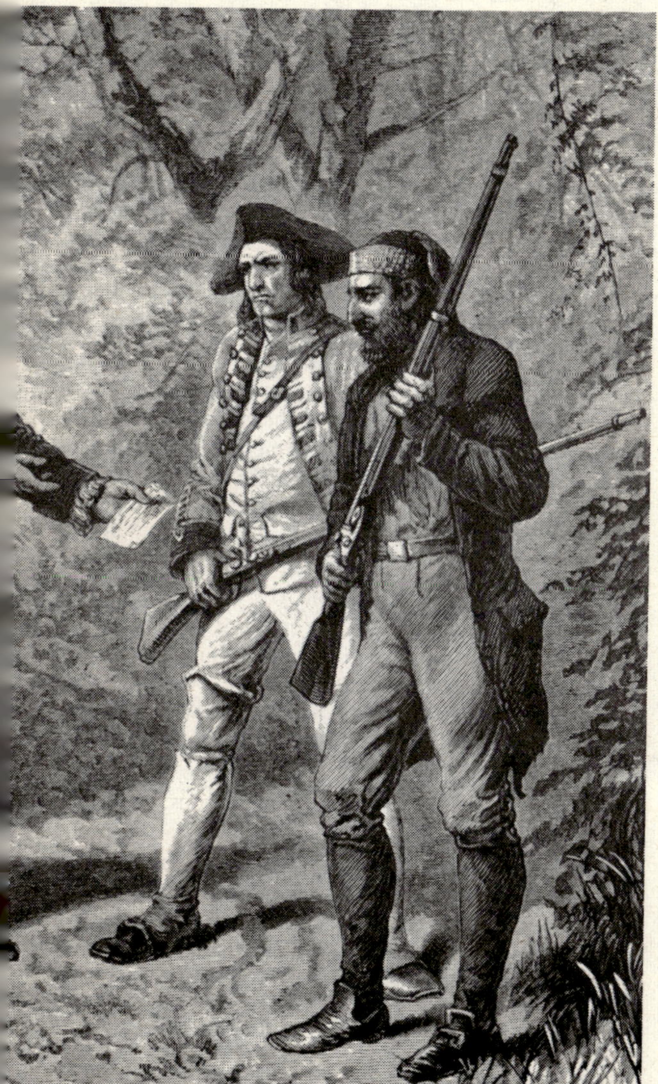

"The unfortunate Colonials are in want of every thing; they have neither coats, nor hats, nor shirts, nor shoes; their feet and legs freeze 'til they grow black, and it is often necessary to amputate them."

Meanwhile in Philadelphia, the British danced. Until May in 1778, there was an unending round of Assembly Balls, theatrical performances, and parties given by Philadelphia's leading Loyalists. All British officers were welcome guests. None were as popular as John André, promoted Major since prisoner exchange returned him to the Royal Fusiliers at about the time of Nathan Hale's execution. Handsome, talented, with enough income to afford the best wines and tailors, he won men's liking while he charmed their womenfolk. Particularly, he seems to have charmed Peggy Shippen, who at barely eighteen was Philadelphia's belle of the season. Properly named Margaret, she was the youngest of three daughters of Justice Edward Shippen, whose family like others long prominent in Philadelphia was divided by the Revolution. His brother, Dr. William Shippen, was chief of the medical department of the Continental Army, while Justice Shippen, though no shouting Loyalist, saw rebellion as a threat to law and order and independence from the Mother Country as a reprehensible dream.

From the first, Peggy and her sisters, Polly and Sally, made the Shippen home a rendezvous for British officers. How often André visited there can only be guessed at. His pencil drawing of Peggy appears to have been the product of several sittings. Other André sketches, including the self-portrait he drew and gave to his executioners, were dashed off quickly; but Peggy's likeness has been re-worked, perhaps to please her by prettifying a petulant mouth and eyes a shade too small, perhaps simply because while she posed and he sketched other callers were turned away. There is something protective in the unanimity with which those who knew them both insisted after the tragedy in which they shared, that their acquaintance was no more than casual.

A blighted love-affair in 1769 had caused André to join the Fusiliers at eighteen. Now twenty-seven but still a romanticist, too fastidious for off-duty philandering, he was at the stage at which their superiors urged rising officers to marry but do so judiciously. One of Peggy Shippen's descendants had no doubt. "Poor André was in love with her. But she refused him, keeping a lock of his hair which we still have." However that stands as evidence, there is ample record that André designed a Turkish costume for her and asked her to wear it at a Mischianza, a fancy-dress ball he arranged to celebrate the coming of Spring in 1778. This was in fact the last grand affair before the French-American alliance and approach of Lafayette with the vanguard of Washington's reinforced and re-equipped army forced the British to evacuate.

In a letter to the *Gentleman's Magazine* in London, André described the ball and named Peggy as his lady of the evening. That she was there was denied, after the British were gone and a rebel journalist commented savagely on "Mischianza ladies equally noted for their Tory principles and their fondness for British debaucheries and macaronies." Shippen family tradition held that their father decided the gossamer costumes André designed were immodest, and forbade Peggy and her sisters to attend. What remains unchallenged is that although they never met again, Peggy and André found means to correspond through the British and American lines; and this brought André and Arnold to their only meeting.

Shortly before André left Philadelphia with the British, Arnold joined Washington at Valley Forge, asking for a combat command. In kindness but fatefully for Arnold, Washington ruled that Arnold's still unhealed and painful wound "would not permit of his services in a more active line," and assigned him to command in Philadelphia. On May 30, 1778, Arnold took the oath newly required of serving officers, declaring "The United States of America to be free, independent and sovereign states," and swearing to "defend the said United States with fidelity according to the best of my skill and understanding." On the same day, André in New York became adjutant-general to Sir Henry Clinton, replacing Sir William Howe as British commander-in-chief, and Arnold in Philadelphia assumed the post that brought Peggy Shippen into his life.

They may have met first at the City Tavern, where "an elegant entertainment was given by the officers of the Continental Army and some Philadelphia patriots, to the young ladies of Philadelphia who had manifested their attachment to the cause of virtue and freedom by sacrificing every convenience to the love of their country"; or at the Old Southwark Theater, where Samuel Adams saw "some American officers condescend to act on the stage while others and one of superior rank (probably Arnold) were pleased to countenance them with their presence." Such British-like frivolities were soon suppressed; Congress passed an emergency resolution that "any person holding an office under the United States who shall act, promote, encourage, or attend such plays shall be deemed unworthy to hold office and shall be accordingly dismissed."

But Arnold by then was caught up in a way of life new and strange to him, and intoxicated by it, and entranced by Peggy Shippen who was its product. "Cupid," Mrs. Robert Morris wrote to her husband, "has given our little General a more mortal wound than all the host of Britons could." To his father, Justice Shippen confided: "My youngest daughter is much solicited by a certain General on the subject of matrimony. Whether this will take place or not depends upon certain circumstances." These circumstances appear to have included prudent paternal concern about the suitor's finances. Writing to him, Arnold said that while he was not rich he was sufficiently well-off to be quite eligible.

This was quite untrue. His pay in depreciated Continental currency was $332 per month. He had no other fixed income, and owned no property but his house in New Haven and a small farm. He had taken over the house and servants and coach-and-four left behind by Sir William Howe, and was hard put to meet the cost. Still somehow he found $500 to send to the children of a friend killed at Bunker Hill, and was otherwise notably generous. Secretly, he borrowed, speculated on risky investments, and unquestionably used his official position to get loans and make a profit where he could. *Post facto,* he was accused of all manner of illegal tricks and stratagems; but the worst that was proved is that he twisted and turned to get money while stopping short of felony, as he had done before in New Haven where sharp practice was deplored but excused if it succeeded. The rule was the same in Philadelphia. Continental currency fell from a third of its face value to a tenth. Businessmen recouped their losses any way they could. The difference Arnold failed or refused to realize was that a public hero has lost his right to privacy.

He must surely have heard much about John André. He was well aware he lacked André's assets that fascinated Peggy Shippen. More than twice her age and weathered older by war and wounds, inches shorter than André and anything but handsome, he lacked social graces, copied his love-letters from a book and still misspelled them, could enter no Philadelphia drawing-room without causing some Philadelphians to leave at the sight of him. And Peggy gave him no encouragement. Still he spent more, speculated more recklessly, and in his single-minded infatuation paid too little heed to his enemies until too late.

On February 9, 1779, the Pennsylvania Council adopted unanimously and sent copies to Congress, Washington, authorities in every state, and the newspapers, a resolution declaring Arnold to be "oppressive to the faithful subjects of this state, unworthy of his rank and station, highly discouraging to those who have manifested their attachment to the liberties and interests of America, and disrespectful to the supreme executive authority." Along with this went a weird melange of accusations, as various as that he had dared to order a prominent civilian's son in uniform to fetch a barber, and that he had invested in a gamble on what a later age would call black-market operations.

No Publick or private Inquiry shall prevail on me to forsake the Cause of my Injur'd & oppressed Country until I see peace & Liberty restored to her, or nobly die in the Attempt. Had any man done more, suffered more, for less reward? Arnold thought not; and a defense attorney could have made out a strong case supporting this belief. He is not defended here. At the time, instead of defending he attacked, demanding a court-martial, and voluntarily resigning command of Philadelphia pending the exculpation he clearly thought would be forthcoming. Like Burgoyne at Saratoga, he caught his attackers by surprise. But greater surprise soon followed. On April 8, Peggy Shippen married him.

His leg gave him such pain, he said, that a soldier must support him during the ceremony, and during the reception that followed he accepted congratulations sitting down with his leg across a camp-stool. His wound was his red badge of courage. From here on, he wore it as his shield. "Before the end of the honeymoon," one historian avers, "Arnold was ready to give up the cause of America." This can be read as a way of saying that Peggy Shippen tempted and the Dark Eagle fell. Which may be true, although until then no man and certainly no woman had been able to buy or sell him. On May 5, he challenged Washington direct: "If your Excellency thinks me criminal, for heaven's sake let me be immediately tried and, if found guilty, executed." He was not in fact charged with anything that invited the death penalty. But on May 10, 1779, within the British lines in New York where Nathan Hale died regretting he had but one life to lose for his country, Arnold's secret emissary told John André that Arnold was ready to turn traitor if the price was right.

André in Philadelphia had known that a certain Joseph Stansbury, a mild-mannered merchant who kept a glass and china shop, was covertly a British spy. Peggy Arnold knew Stansbury. Arnold did not. But Stansbury bore Arnold's offer of services "in any way that would most effectually restore the former government and destroy the usurped authority of Congress, either by immediately joining the British Army or co-operating on some concealed plan with Sir Henry Clinton." André was not Clinton's spymaster. But from the beginning Arnold dealt only with André; and Peggy's correspondence makes it clear she promoted this relationship. It is impossible to believe all was coincidental or impromtu. The mystery is: Which of the three controlled, and with what ultimate objective?

André sent word that it would be best for Arnold to continue in the Continental Army, obtaining and forwarding secret information. He would write to Peggy Arnold's friend, Peggy Chew. Her answers written in good faith would be given to Peggy Arnold, to be forwarded to André. Peggy Arnold would interline Peggy Chew's letters with reports from Arnold written in invisible ink. "This will come by a flag of truce, etc., every messenger remaining ignorant of

The capture of Fort Ticonderoga. (Culver)

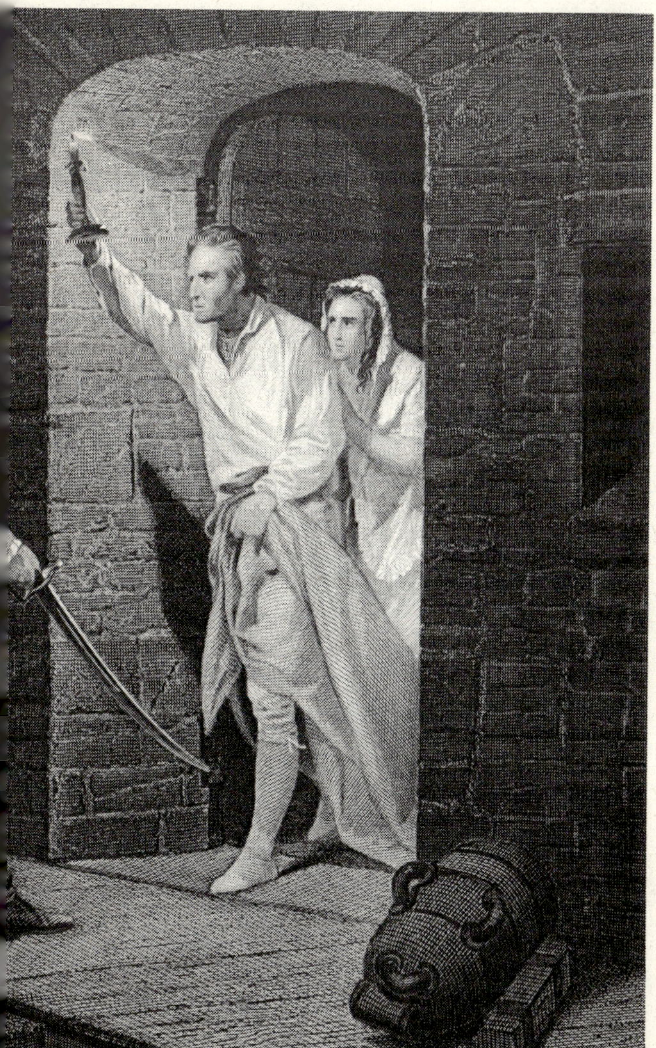

what they are charged with. The letters may talk of the Mischianza or some other nonsense." Supporting proposed pretense, André wrote: "It would make me very happy to become useful to you here. You know the Mischianza made me a complete milliner. Should you not have received supplies for your fullest equipment for that department, I shall be glad to enter the whole detail of cap-wire, needles, gauze, &c., and, to the best of my ability, render you in these trifles services from which I hope you would infer a zeal to be further employed." Primly, Peggy replied: "Mrs. Arnold begs leave to assure Captain André that her friendship and esteem for him is not impaired by time or accident." One can only wonder what Arnold read between such lines.

Congress continued to delay his court-martial, while dictating strategy to Washington and juggling his Generals. Letters went back and forth between Arnold and André. A motley cast of characters entered the melodrama: preachers, poets, deserters, double agents, their espionage and treason variously masked. Arnold demanded guarantees that André could not or would not give; Clinton as André's superior demanded guarantees Arnold would only imply. At long last, his court-martial began, and Arnold rushed to the attack as heedlessly as he charged at Freeman's Farm and Bemis Heights. But now the adversaries were civilians, who scattered but re-formed. Four of the charges against Arnold were dropped; on the others, he was convicted. Congress ordered Washington to reprimand him publicly. Obeying, Washington in effect apologized. But Arnold was unappeased.

Months had dragged by, and still neither he nor André were committed past the point of no retreat. Now Arnold wrote that he had been given command of West Point, and would sell it, and British control of the Hudson, for £20,000, cash on delivery. Actually, he had only asked General Philip Schuyler to help him get the West Point assignment; and all seemed lost when Washington, meaning to show his confidence in Arnold was uimpaired, summoned him back to active duty, to command the left wing of the Continental Army in attack across the Hudson. For the first and last time, Arnold demurred from battle and the chance for glory. Pleading his three-year-old wound as excuse, he gained what he must have to earn his pay from the British: orders from Washington to "proceed to West Point and take the command of that post and its dependencies."

Leaving Peggy in Philadelphia, he hurried to West Point. In New York, Clinton and André debated: Should André, or some hireling who could be spared if things went wrong, go to close the bargain with Arnold? André said he knew Arnold and understood him, though they had never met; and only he could make sure that Arnold would bely his reputation by dealing honestly. Clinton gave in, and André hurried off to complete a comedy he had written in Mischianza style. It had three performances, the last on the evening of André's capture inside the Continental Army's lines. And this capture climaxed a mystery-drama whose *deus ex machina* was also its author: Arnold. By moonlight on the night of September 21, 1780, at Stony Point overlooking the Hudson, he and André met for the first time, but not as strangers. There were no witnesses to their colloquy, that went on until 4 in the morning. Then Arnold guided André to where he said a boat would be waiting to take André back to the British ship *Vulture* anchored in midstream. There was no boat. Arnold expressed surprise and concern, but said André need not worry, and led to two saddled horses. Riding side-roads, they passed a sentry. André realized he was inside the Continental Army's lines. This, he swore when all was over, was "against my stipulation,

The execution of Nathan Hale. (Culver)

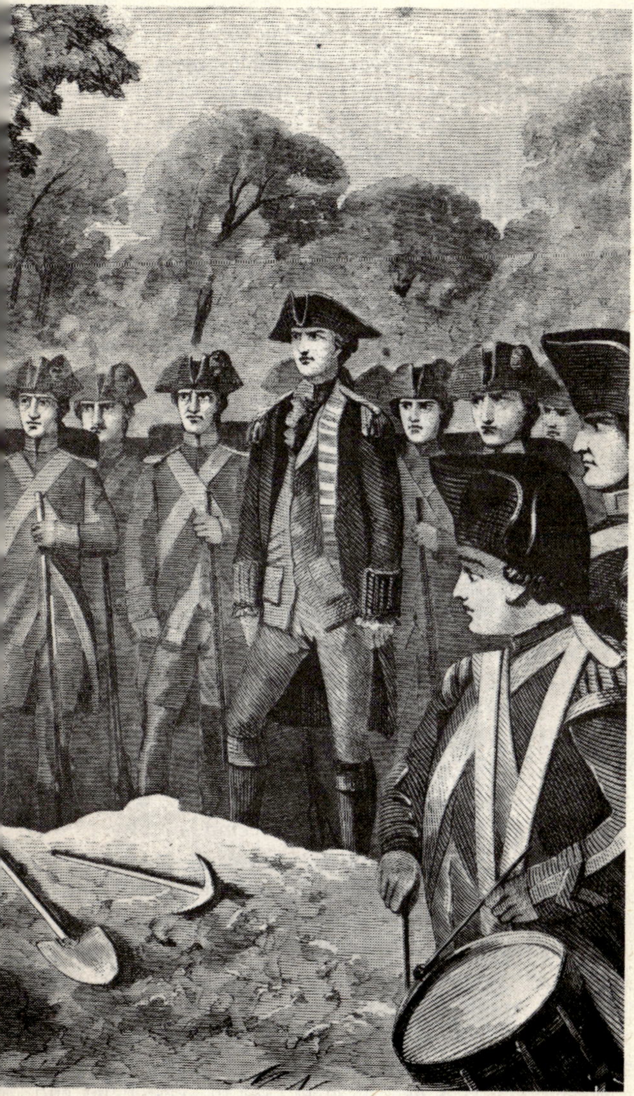

my intention, and without my knowledge beforehand."

But turning back was impossible; he must follow where Arnold led. This was, first, to a house from which in the morning they watched a shore-battery open fire on the *Vulture* and force its Captain to lift anchor and drop down-river. Arnold said the battery fired without his orders. He must go and see about this. Meanwhile André would be guided by trustworthy persons, to safety in New York. He would, however, have to take off his uniform and go disguised as a civilian. André protested. Arnold was firm. He rode away, to join Peggy at West Point, and learned from her that staff-officers had "begged her to use her influence" to dissuade him from further meetings with persons suspected of smuggling. She knew who the suspects were, and what they were in reality. If she guessed that André was in danger, it was already too late to save him.

On September 23, André and Arnold's guide reached a bridge over the Croton River. At that point, the guide left him to ride alone toward the British lines at White Plains 15 miles farther on. Riding down Hardscrabble Road past Chappaqua and Pleasantville, André turned off in the direction of Tarrytown. At another bridge, three Westchester volunteers lay in wait for whatever might pass by; a recent New York ordinance gave them authority to claim as prize any property they might find on a captured enemy. John Paulding, Isaac Van Wart and David Williams stopped André on suspicion, searched him looking for legal loot, and found hidden in his boot the papers that made him technically a spy.

This news reached Arnold and Peggy while they prepared to entertain Washington at breakfast, on September 25. Arnold "went upstairs to his lady," soon came down again "in great confusion and, ordering a horse to be saddled, mounted him and said to inform General Washington that he was gone over to West Point and would return in about an hour." Then Arnold rode pellmell to refuge aboard the *Vulture*. Washington, still uninformed of André's capture, arrived, breakfasted, expressed regret at having missed Arnold, and departed. Then staff-officers "heard a shriek, ran upstairs, and there met Mrs. Arnold raving distracted. Her morning gown with few other clothes remained on her —too few to be seen by strangers." A doctor was called. "We carried her to her bed, raving mad."

Alexander Hamilton pitied her. So did almost everyone. And as many pitied André, while all cursed Arnold; all but André, who blamed no one but himself, spoke not a word about Peggy, and adjusted the hangman's rope around his neck while Arnold was collecting payment for his treason. *A miserable bargainer?* Commissioned a Brigadier General in the British Army, granted £6,315 as compensation for property he claimed he lost by leaving the Continental Army, he cried for more, and got it; a pension for Peggy who joined him in England, allowances and military rank for his three sons, and opportunity to strike back at the civilians he blamed for driving him to treason. Again, he led troops, but not in combat; at the head of British forays, he ordered the burning of Richmond and destroyed a part of New London. In December, 1781, he was in London, consulted on American affairs by George III and the British ministry. But the manner of André's death weighed against him, and officers and gentlemen declined to serve with a traitor of whatever stripe. With the Revolution over, the United States established, he was at home nowhere. He tried trading from Canada to the West Indies, failed, returned to England, briefly saw hope of action when war broke out between Great Britain and France but was not wanted in any capacity, and "gradually sank into melancholy and slowly died." Peggy Arnold was with him to the end. He had seen to it that she had nowhere else to go.

In December, 1863, the Atlantic Monthly published *The Man Without a Country,* a short story by Nathan Hale's grand-nephew, Edward Everett Hale, then pastor of Boston's South Congregational Church. A month before, Edward Everett Hale was orator of the day at Gettysburg and spoke for two hours, after which Abraham Lincoln offered brief remarks hardly noticed at the time but treasured today as the Gettysburg Address. Hale's story, a classic for a century, tells of an invented character who cursed the United States and shouted "I wish I may never hear of the United States again." Hale named his protagonist Philip Nolan. There was a real Philip Nolan, who died heroically in trying to add Texas to the United States, in November, 1800. The only monument to Nolan is a highway marker which identifies him as "a horse trader whose name was immortalized in E. E. Hale's *The Man Without a Country.*" Forever, Nolan's name is affixed to Hale's epitaph for a Philip Nolan who never existed: "He loved his country as no other man has loved her; but no man deserved less at her hands." Just possibly, this sums the secret history of Benedict Arnold.

CONTRIBUTORS

Robert Hardy Andrews has contributed fourteen articles to MANKIND in the past five years. Among his published books are *A Corner of Chicago, Burning Gold, Little Big Mouth, Great Day in the Morning,* and his biography of Madame Pandit, *A Lamp for India.*

G. G. Hatheway is a graduate of Yale University. Dr. Hatheway lectures on American history at Purdue University.

Cecil B. Currey received his Ph.D. from the University of Kansas and is presently associate professor of Early American History and Culture as well as Chairman of the History Graduate Program at the University of South Florida.

Robert Sobel is associate professor of history at the New College of Hofstra. He is the author of several books including *Prosperity on Margin: The Stock Market in the 1920s.*

A graduate of the University of Virginia, Howald Baily is a freelance writer and public relations consultant. He lives in New York City.

Mikhail Belov heads the geography and history department of the Arctic and Antarctic Scientific Research Institute at Leningrad. He is a graduate of Leningrad University, Russia.

David Lindsey is professor of history at California State College, Los Angeles. He is the author of five books on American history.

Mankind Is America's Liveliest and Most Beautiful Magazine of History!
Subscribe Now!

Each new issue of Mankind magazine brings you the delight of discovering fresh, bold, unexpected ideas relating to man's adventure on earth. You may join the Knights Templars crusading to free the Holy Land in one article, then thrill to Lord Byron's vision of the glory that was Greece in another. You could visit with Catherine the Great of Russia, travel in the western badlands with Jesse James, explore the London slums of Hogarth's England or battle with Grant at Vicksburg. The writing is lively. The subjects fascinating. The format bold and dynamic. Priceless photographs, authentic maps and drawings and magnificent art in full color illustrate articles written by the world's foremost historians and authors. Mankind is the most entertaining and rewarding magazine you and your family can read. Discover the pleasure of reading Mankind now. Your introductory subscription rate is only $5 for the full 6-issue year.

SUBSCRIPTION FORM • MAIL TODAY

MANKIND PUBLISHING CO., Dept. MKB
8060 MELROSE AVE., LOS ANGELES, CALIF. 90046

Gentlemen: Please enter my subscription to Mankind Magazine for the full subscription year.

☐ Enclosed is check, cash or money order for $5
☐ Please bill me

Name_____

Address_____

City_____

State_____ Zip_____

MANKIND BOOKS ORDER FORM

MANKIND PUBLISHING CO., Dept. MKB
8060 MELROSE AVE., LOS ANGELES, CALIF. 90046

Please send me the books indicated below for which I enclose $_____ ☐ check, ☐ money order, ☐ cash, payment in full.

CURRENT TITLES @ $1.75 each

_____ copy(ies) THE ANCIENT WORLD
_____ copy(ies) GREAT MILITARY CAMPAIGNS
_____ copy(ies) THE AMERICAN INDIAN
_____ copy(ies) THE HUMAN SIDE OF HISTORY.
_____ copy(ies) BIRTH OF AMERICA
_____ copy(ies) THE AMERICAN WEST
_____ copy(ies) THE CIVIL WAR
_____ copy(ies) GREAT MILITARY BATTLES

NOTE: Enclose 25c additional per order to help cover the cost of shipping and handling. California residents add 5% tax.

Name_____

Address_____

City_____

State_____ Zip_____

GREAT ADVENTURES OF HISTORY

These books, produced in the image of Mankind Magazine, provided interesting reading on a variety of fascinating subjects grouped to a singular theme in each volume. You will enjoy reading all books in this series and, in addition, find the varied subject matter, the quality production and visual beauty make these books ideal gifts for any occasion.